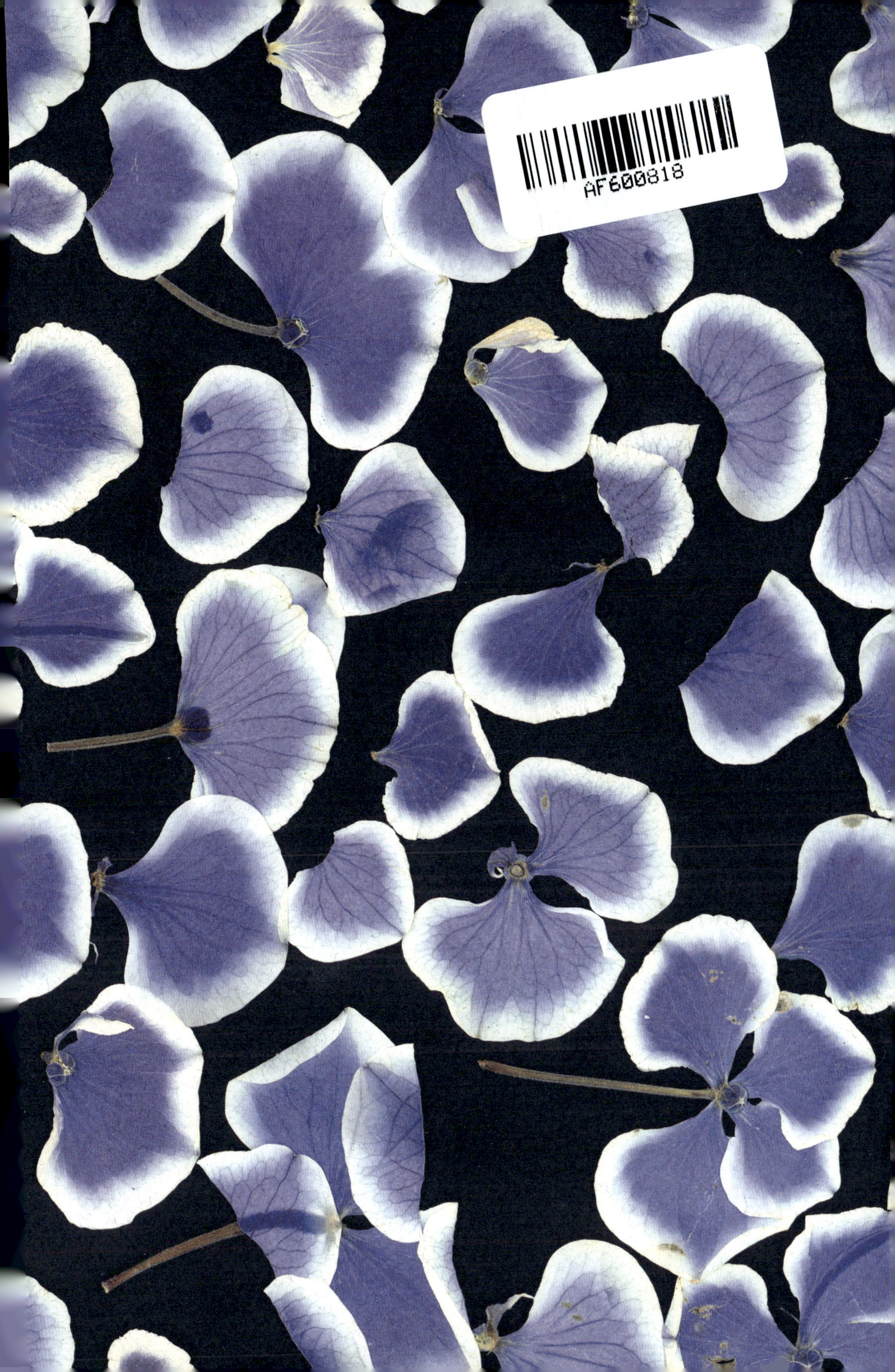

AF600818

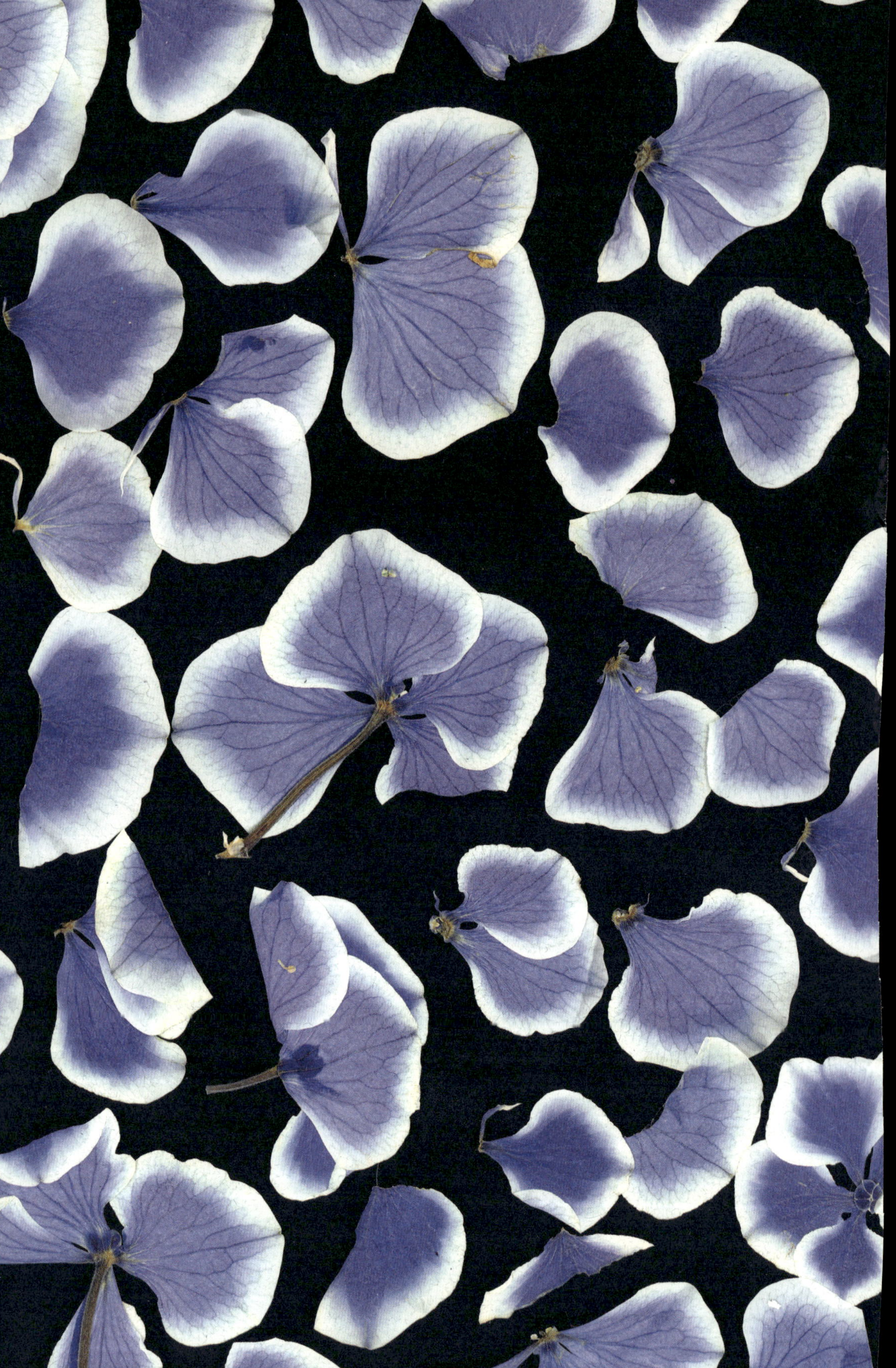

Benny Nemer

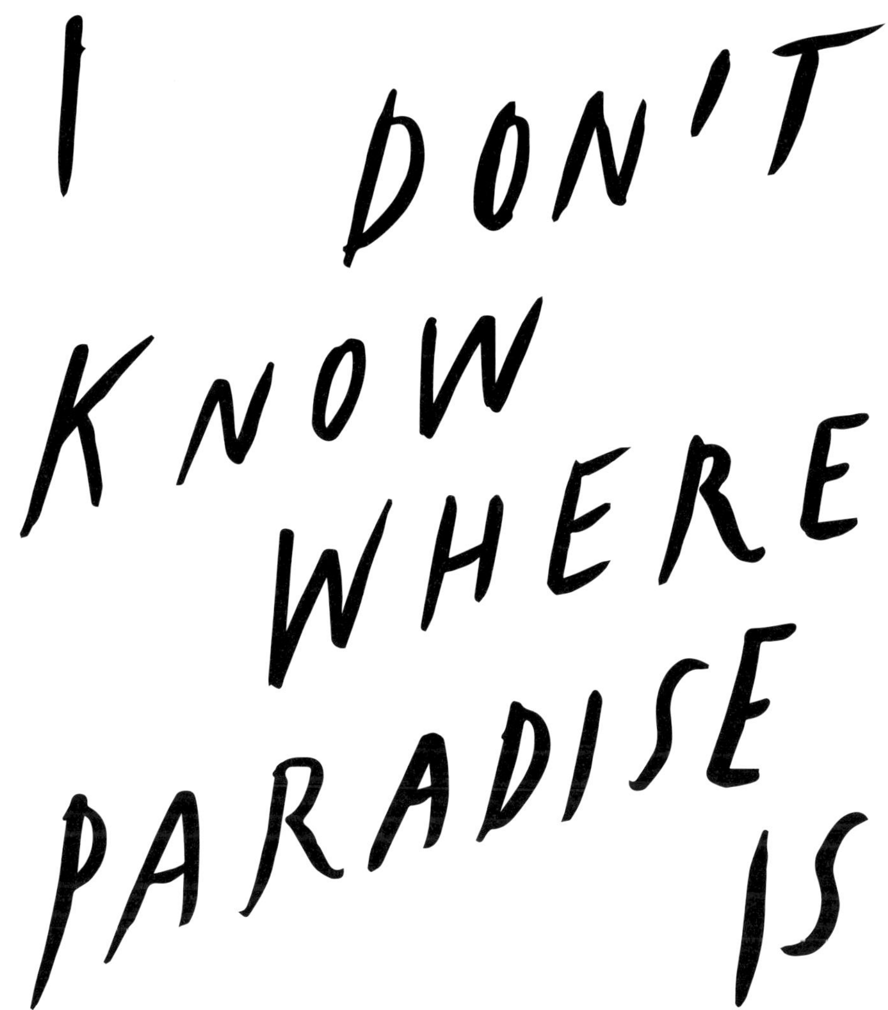

Texts by Heather Anderson
Ann Cvetkovich Jennifer Evans
John Potvin

Carleton University
Art Gallery

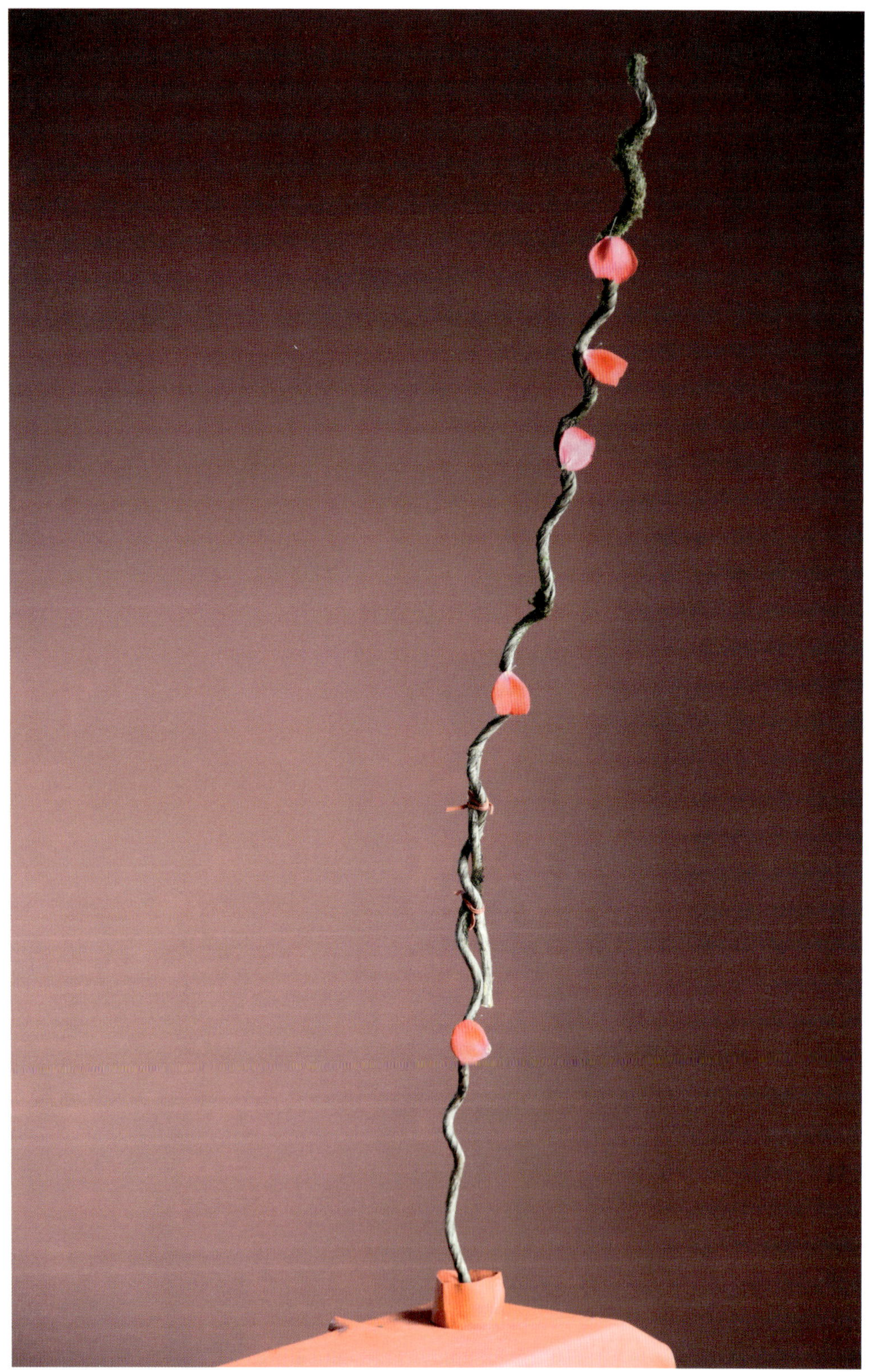

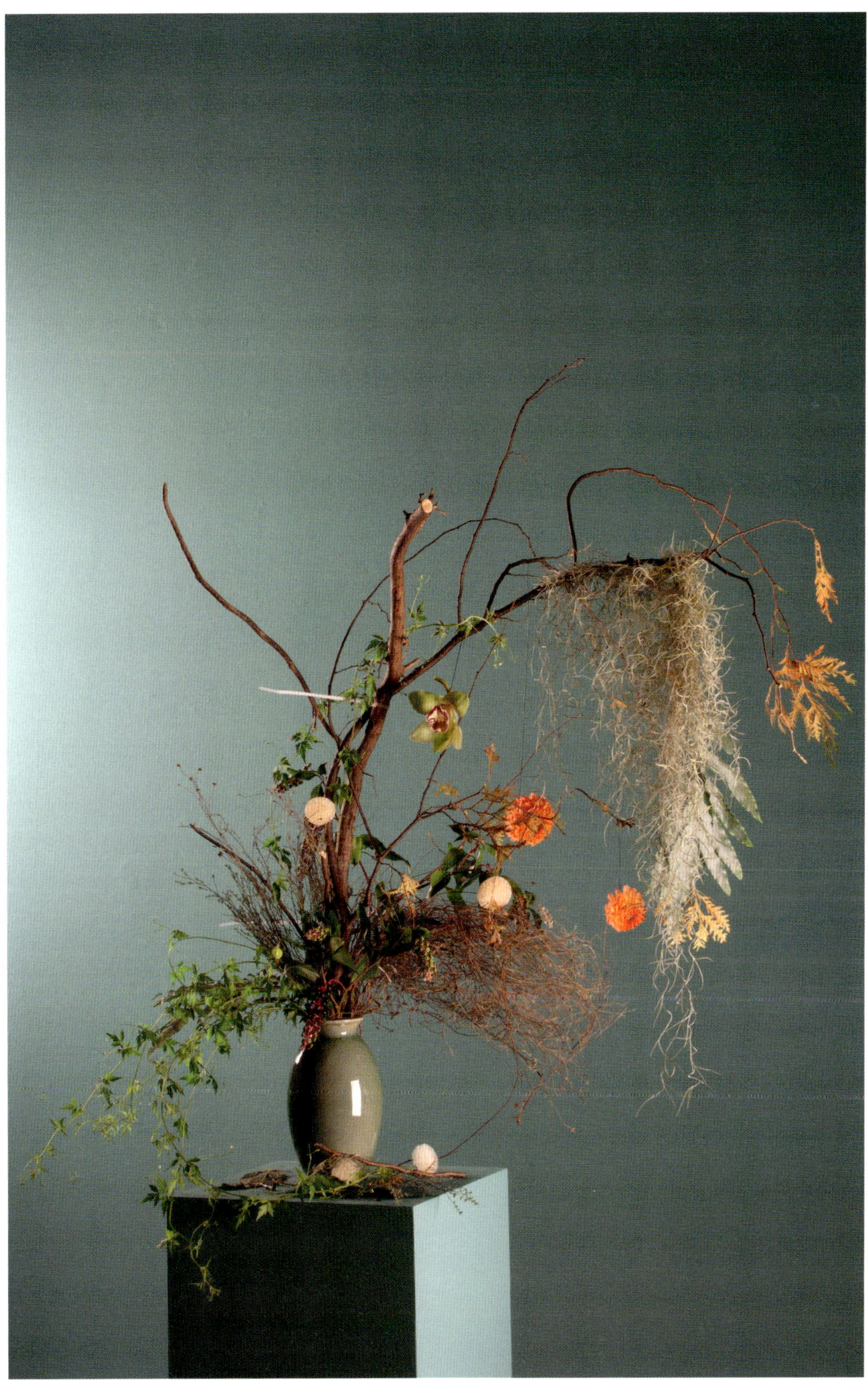

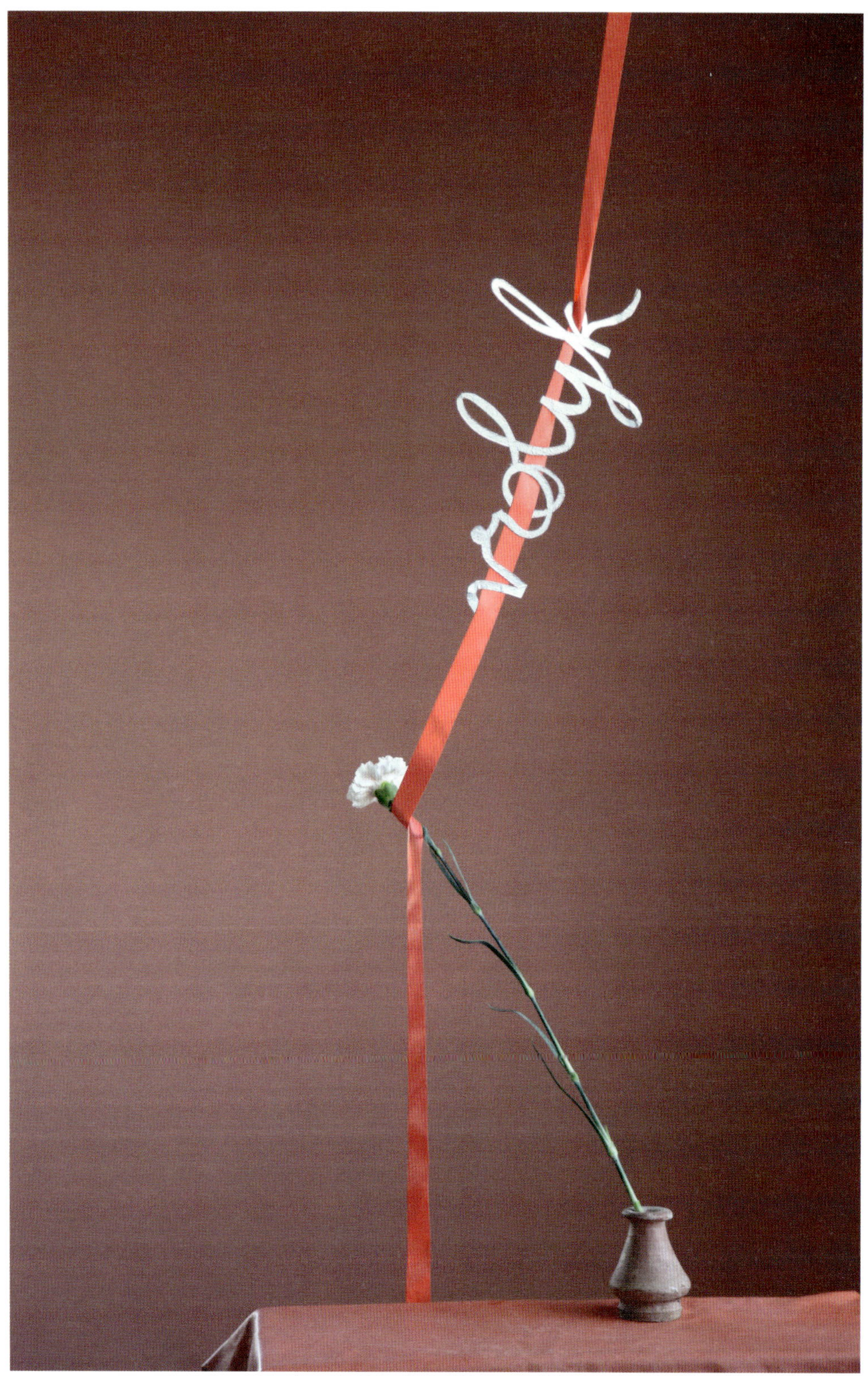

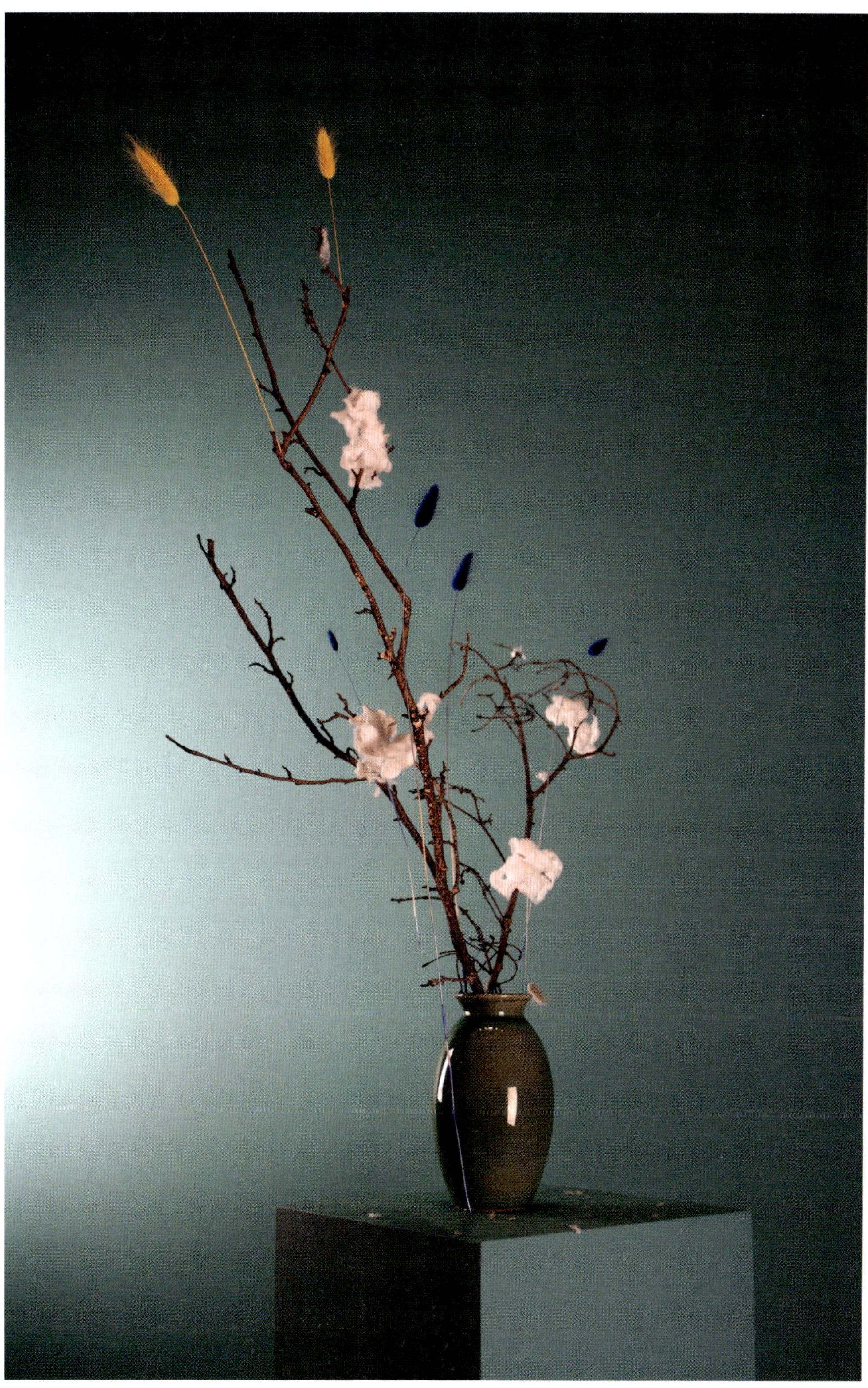

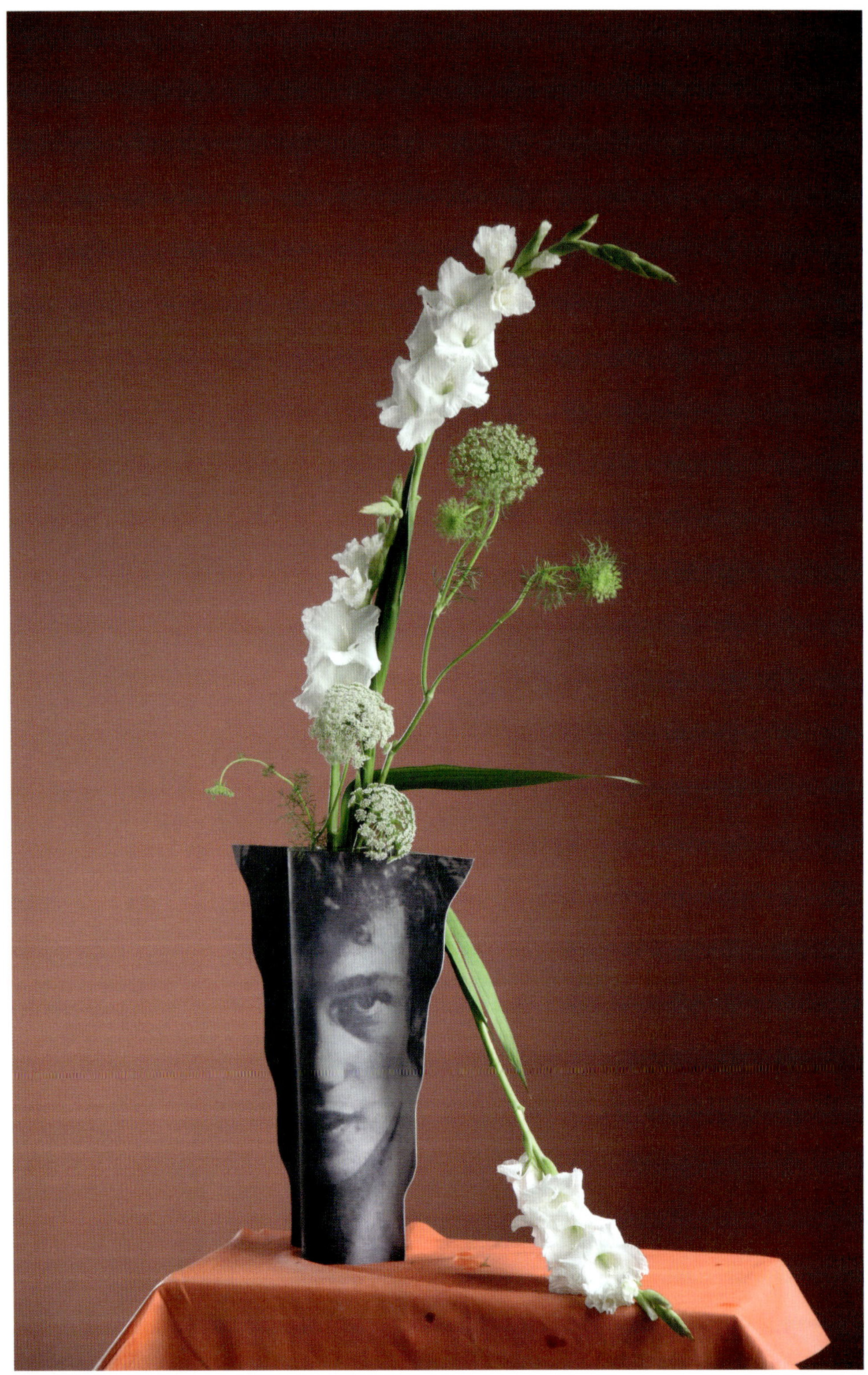

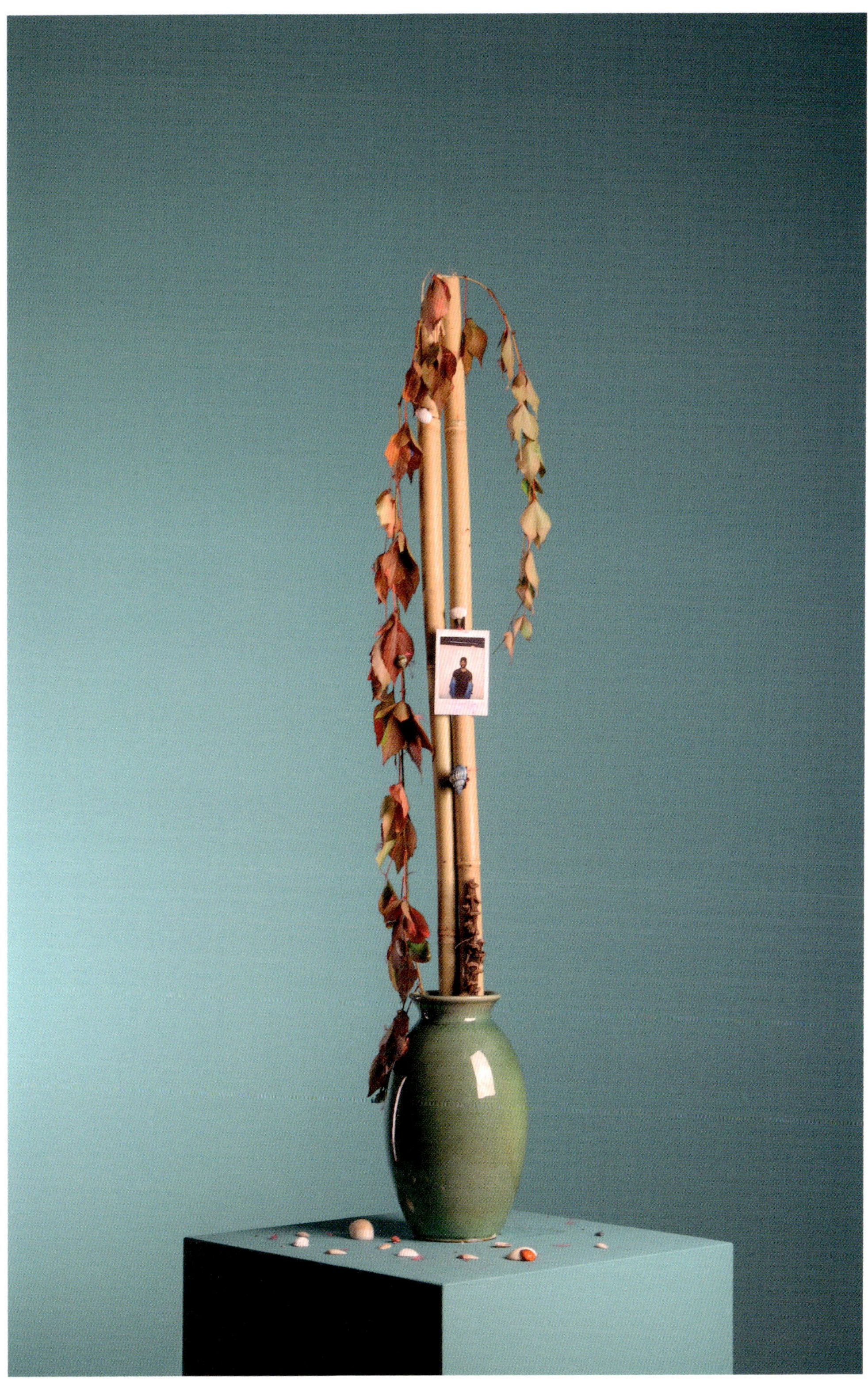

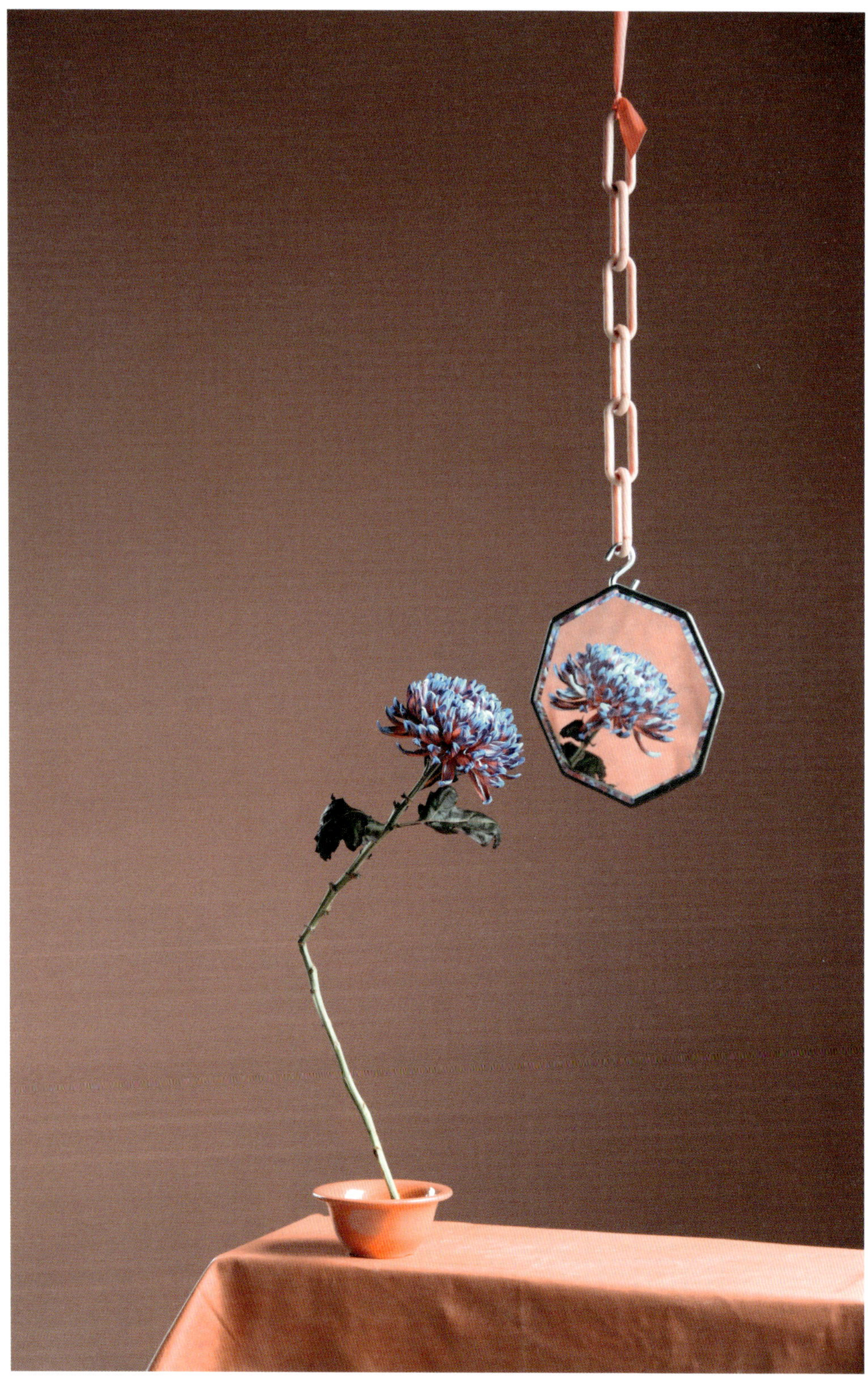

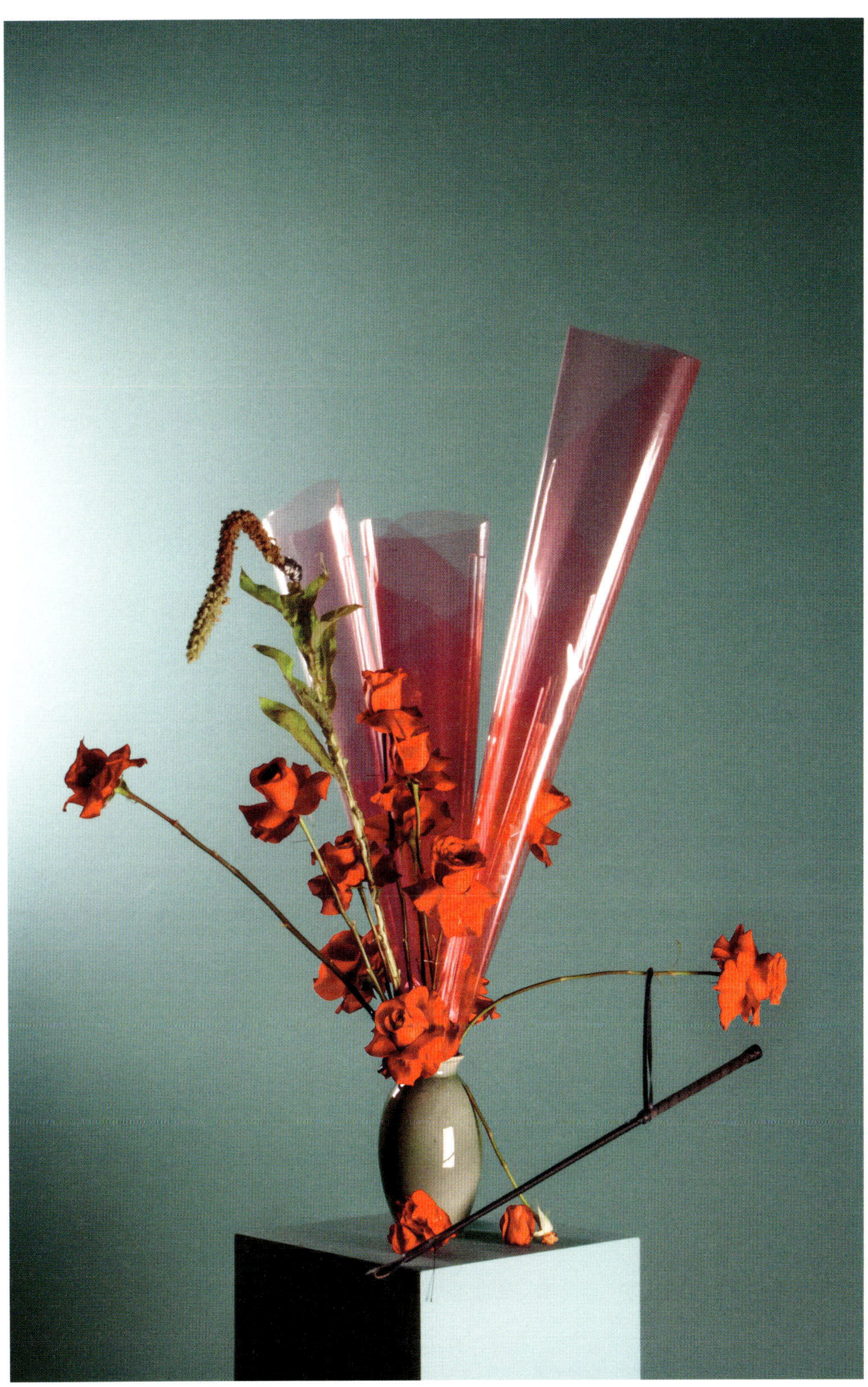

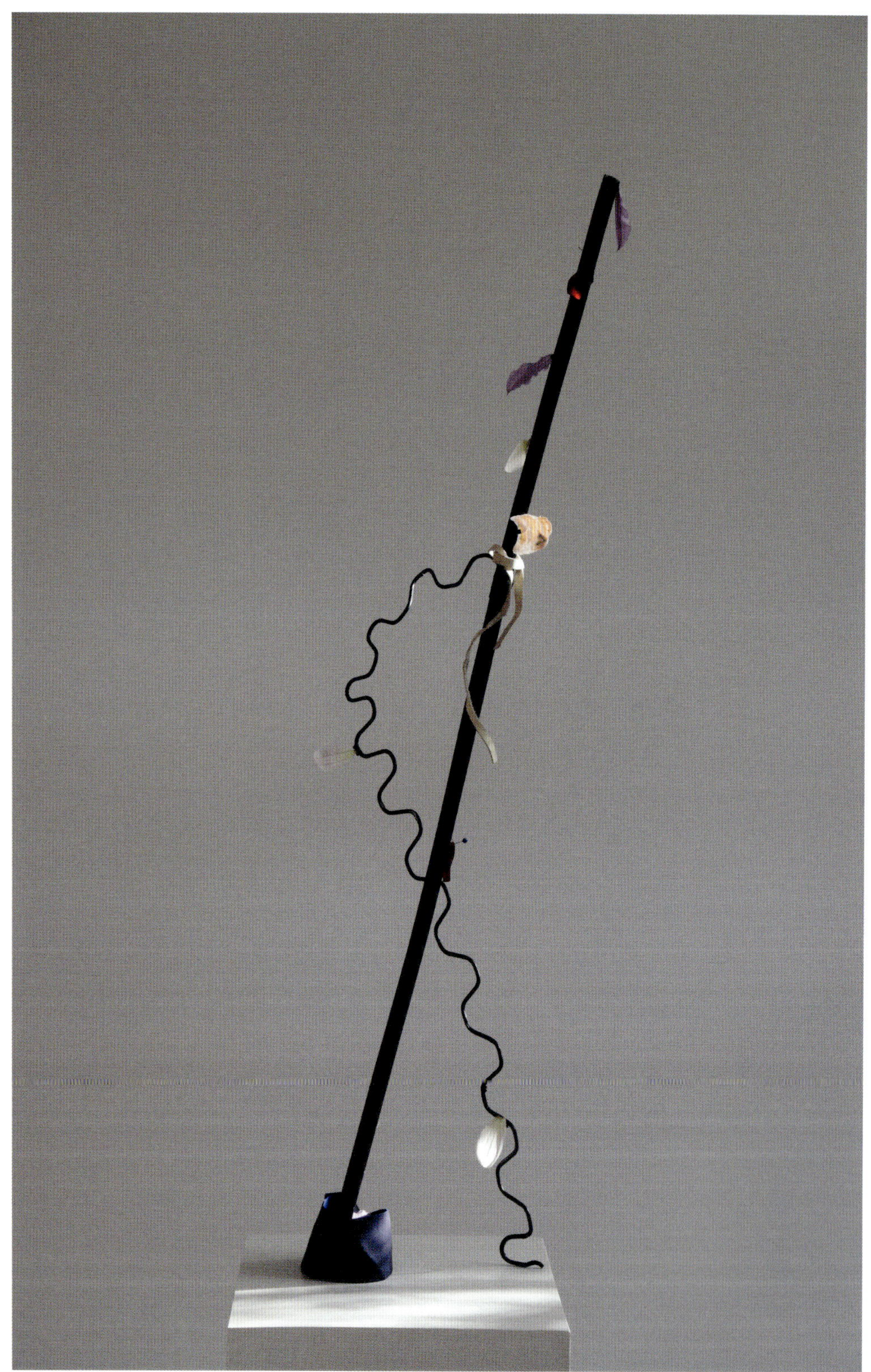

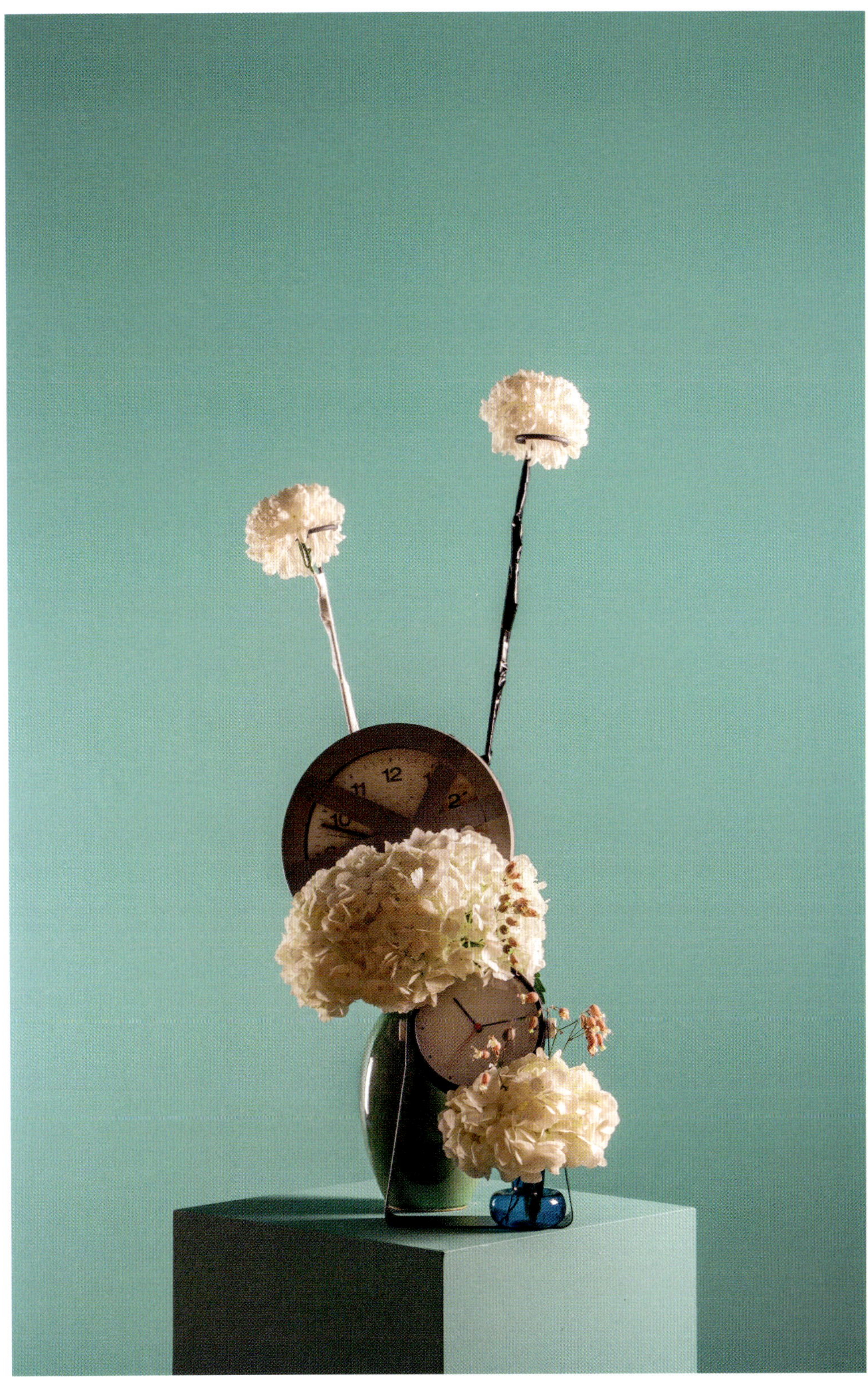

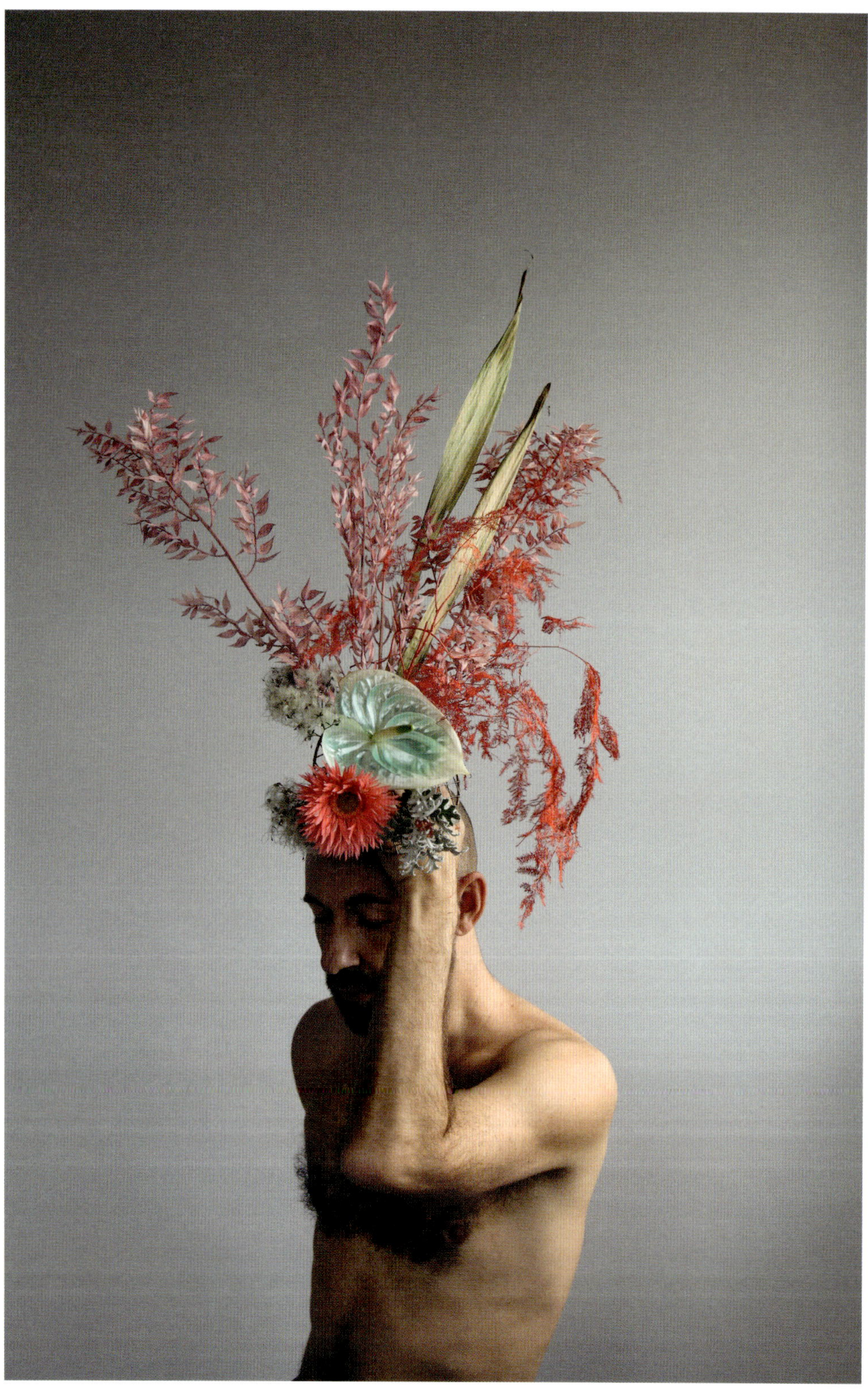

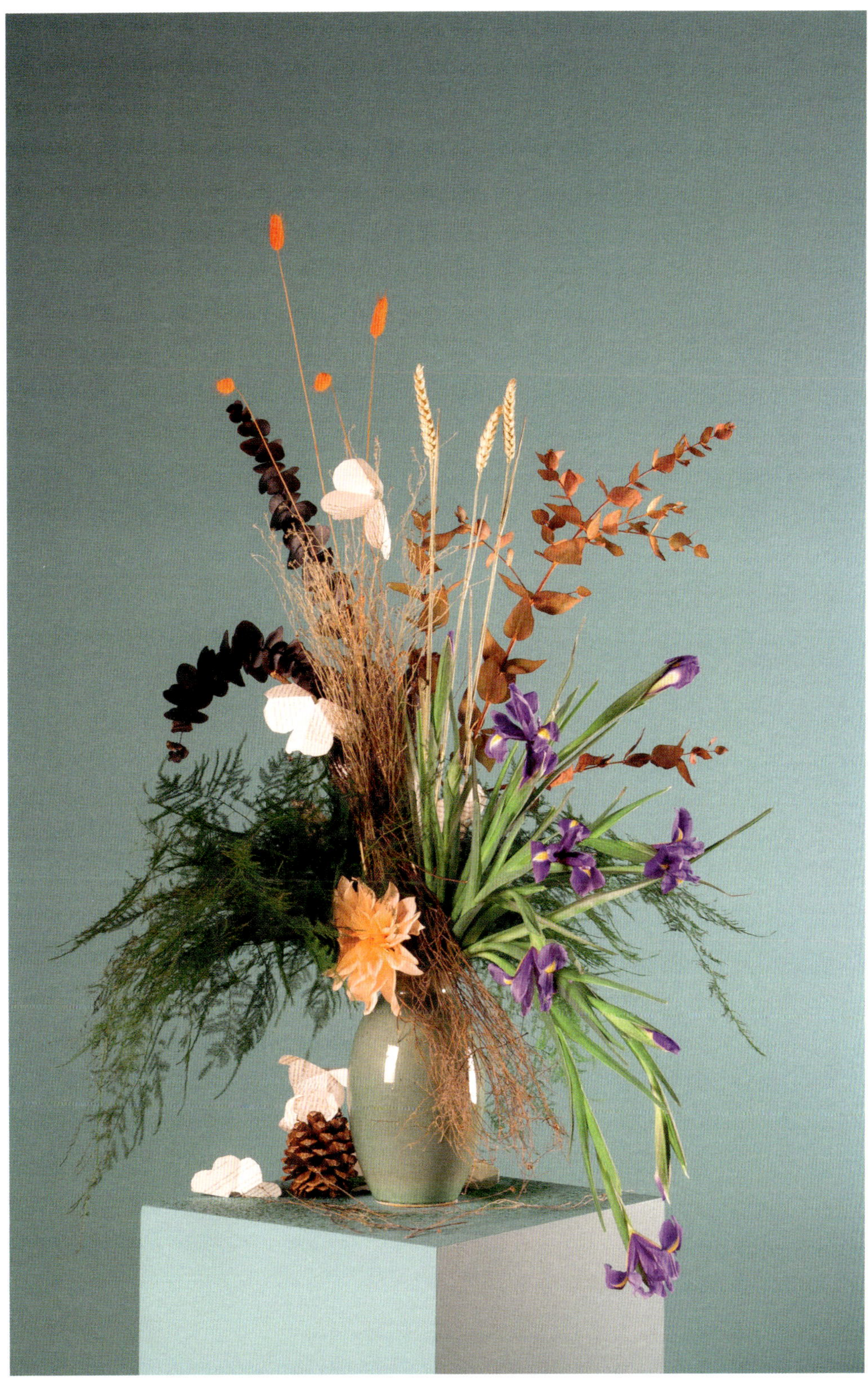

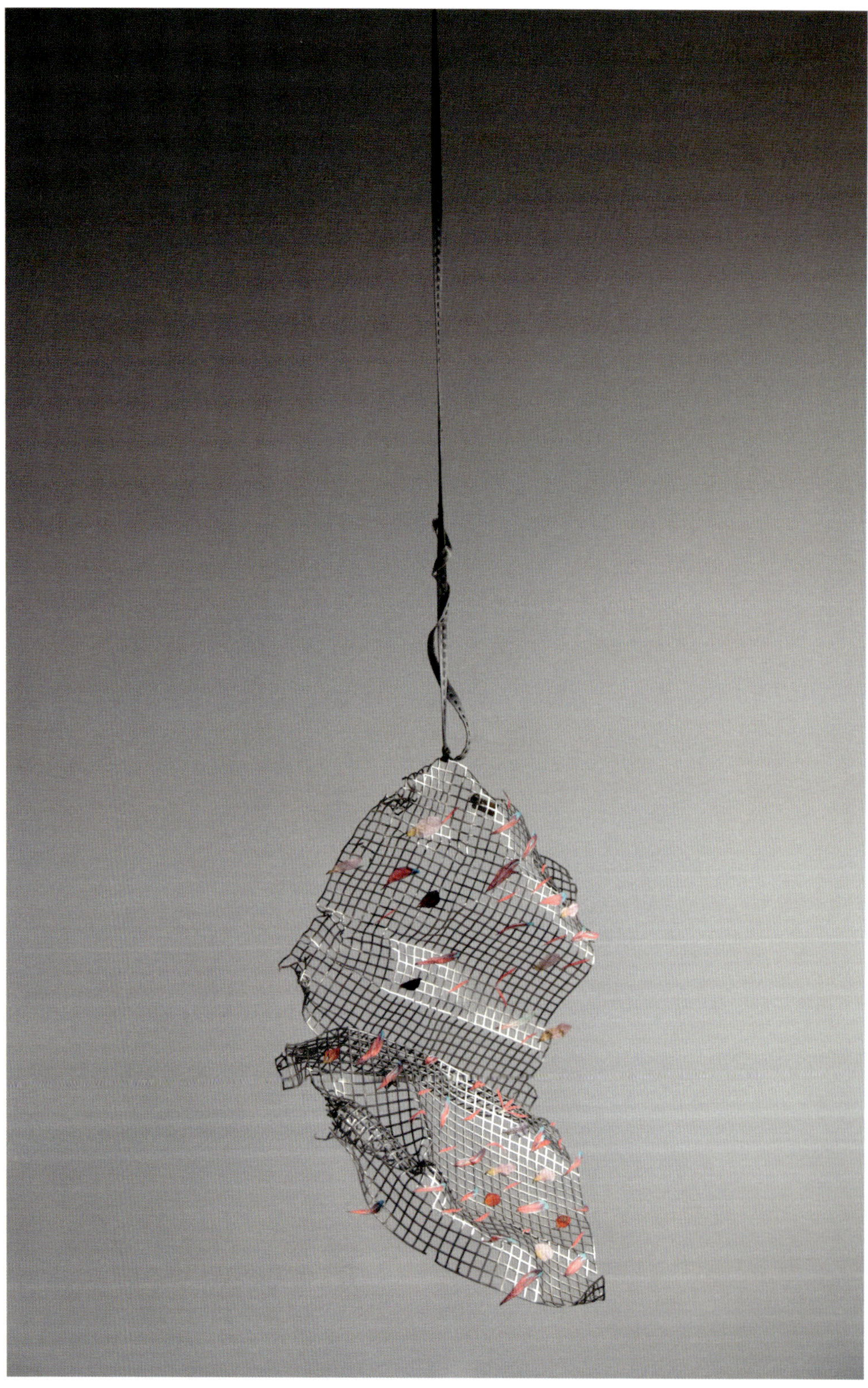

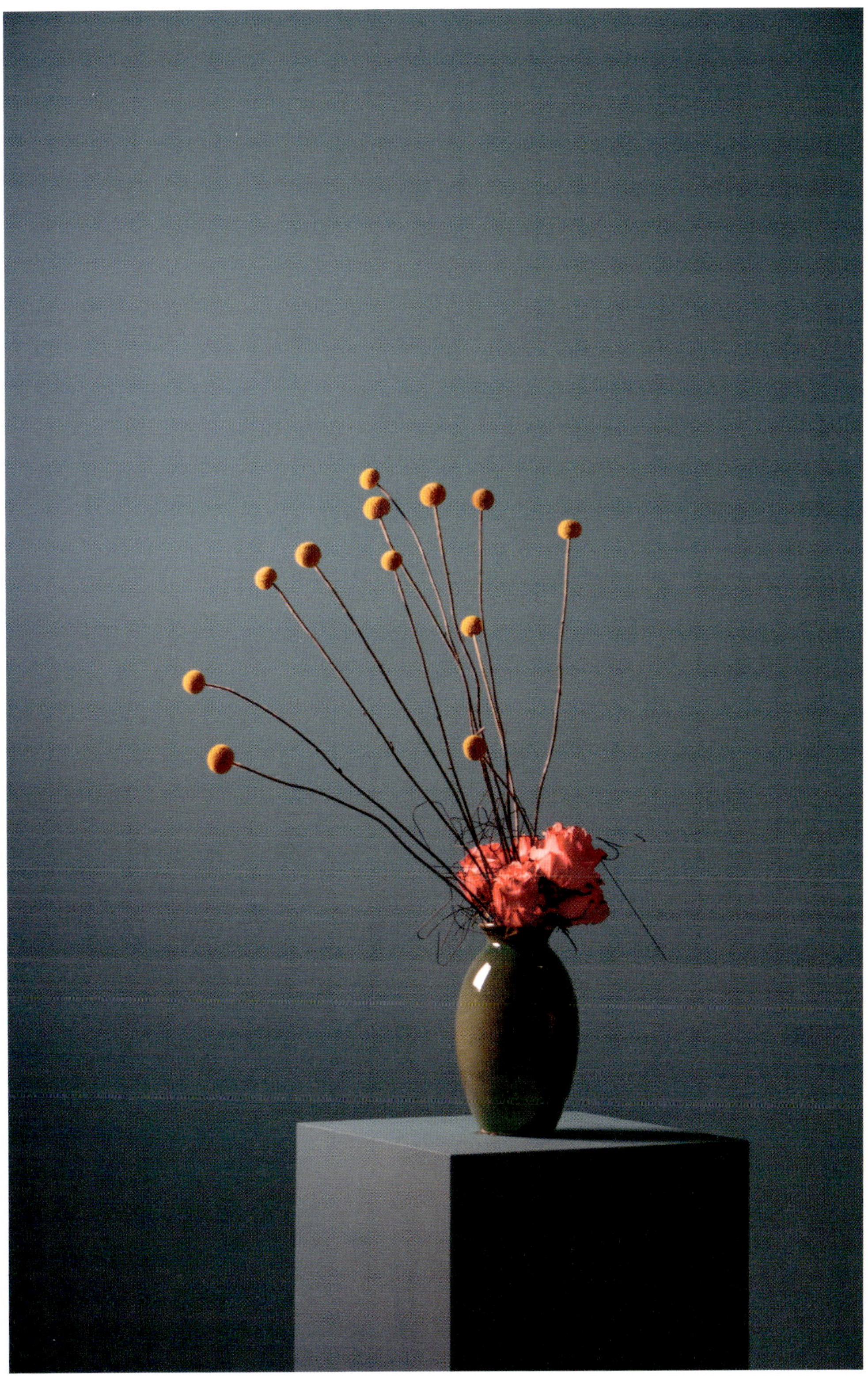

CONTENTS

Handwritten excerpts from the *I Don't Know Where Paradise Is* audio work appear on pages 25–26; 43–44; 55–56; 71–72; 97–98

TO MOVE WITH US: *I DON'T KNOW WHERE PARADISE IS* AS HETEROTOPIA

HEATHER ANDERSON

Adrian and Denis's library is wallpapered with a pattern of branches, acorns, birds and butterflies… it is a short walk through an arch of white clematis to their garden, which is itself filled with flowers, branches and a variety of birds. Plants with long histories climb the bookshelves and hang from the staircases of Tom's library, and his roof terrace is surrounded by boxelder trees.[1]

A lilting male voice narrates this description of two domestic libraries. The text is found in a chapter of Benny Nemer's *I Don't Know Where Paradise Is*, an audio work that transports listeners to the personal libraries of a loosely associated group of elder gay scholars in Amsterdam, London, Montreal, Paris and Vienna. The voices of Nemer and a chorus of other narrators accompany listeners through a labyrinth of books, objects, plants, characters, histories and ideas, with a focus on the Amsterdam library of Gert Hekma and Mattias Duyves.

Distilled from Nemer's research and experiences of these libraries, the audio work's hour-long composition is randomized, drawing from twenty-five chapters to offer a unique listening experience each time the work is accessed. Nemer conjures figures, knowledge and feelings from the queer past, present and future and invites prospective listeners to tune in to the hum of the library, "to move with us, to move your eyes across a page of printed text, to move your body from room to room, to move through time, and in doing so, to move something inside yourself."[2]

Nemer's audio work grounded his exhibition *I Don't Know Where Paradise Is*, presented by Carleton University Art Gallery

(CUAG) in autumn 2020. Each week, Nemer chose a chapter of the work as the inspiration for two floral arrangements: one created by Nemer in his Paris studio, and another by a member of Ottawa's Two-Spirit, Lesbian, Gay, Bisexual, Transgender, Queer+ community and presented in an elegant green vase on a green plinth against a green wall at CUAG. Photographs of the Paris and Ottawa floral arrangements were brought together as a diptych on the gallery's website and shared on social media along with a link to the related audio chapter.

Audiences could listen to Nemer's audio work while looking at images of the floral arrangements online from home, or perhaps on a smartphone during a walk, or when visiting CUAG to directly experience one of the extraordinary arrangements—when it was feasible to do so amid Covid-19 closures. Although the audio work was to have been only one part of a long-anticipated survey exhibition of Nemer's work at CUAG, we radically reimagined the project,[3] such that the audio work and accompanying floral arrangements became *the* exhibition, accessible by anyone with internet access.

Writing now, in the summer of 2022, I have been reflecting on how *I Don't Know Where Paradise Is*—the audio work and the exhibition—resonated with audiences during what we now know was an early phase of the pandemic. That the exhibition functioned across geographies and temporalities and could be engaged incrementally via social media, in person at CUAG and as the audio and visual archive accrued on the CUAG website—all while Nemer and CUAG collaborated with community members in actualizing the exhibition over three months—constituted for

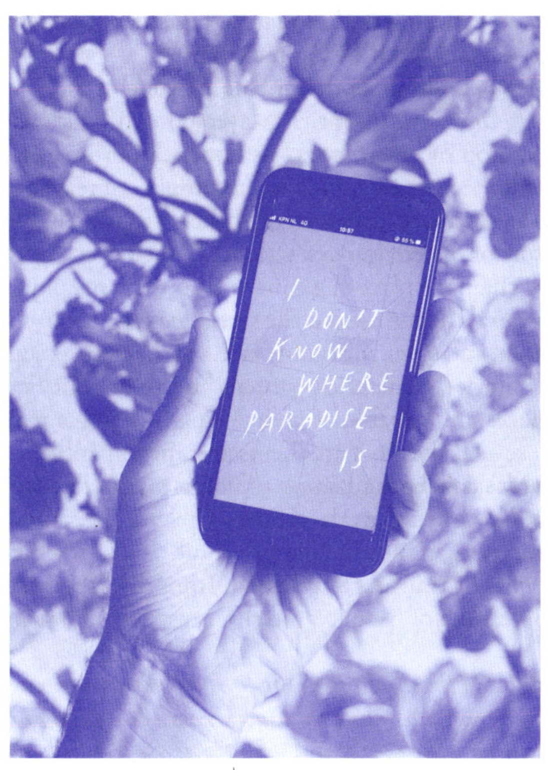

The chapters of I Don't Know Where Paradise Is *are housed on a mobile app that shuffles a unique sequence of the audio material for each listener. Photo: Benny Nemer.*

CUAG a new, experimental model for artist-led, collaborative and community-engaged exhibition making.

This new exhibition model and the artworks at the core of *I Don't Know What Paradise Is* offer richly layered manifestations of Michel Foucault's notion of heterotopia. As Foucault outlined in a Culture française radio lecture in 1966,[4] a heterotopia is a real space that we experience as set apart, different or "other" from daily life and that creates "a sort of mixed, joint experience,"[5] such that one might experience more than one place at a time within the same physical space.[6] Foucault created the term from the Greek *heteros*, meaning different, other, another, and *topos*, meaning place. His heterotopology includes museums, libraries, cemeteries, gardens and so on. For Foucault, heterotopic spaces are "capable of juxtaposing in a single real space several spaces, several sites that are themselves incompatible."[7]

Foucault's conceptualization of libraries as heterotopias, where tangible books offer portals to other places, becomes a virtual deep-listening experience in Nemer's audio work, in which his evocative descriptions transport audiences from diverse physical spaces to share something of his encounters with specific libraries:

> *Crossing the threshold into the library, you are greeted by a sign with a few lines of Dutch verse. It is high on the wall just past the coat stand where you are free to leave your jacket or your bag or whatever you brought with you. The title of the poem, "Vrolijk," means cheerful in the classical sense of happy and gay...* "Long live gay and lesbian literature, in this accomplished piece of architecture. Only water and fire are sins against nature here." *From a far neighbour...*[8]

As exemplified by the excerpt from "A Line of Dutch Verse" above, the narration of each chapter is inviting, conjuring the library as a welcoming space. In another chapter, "A *Ficus drupacea pubescens*," a woman's voice slowly describes the way this distinctive plant occupies the sitting room of Gert Hekma and Mattias Duyves's library, its teardrop-shaped leaves touching the sofa, a painting of irises, the carpet and a nearby shelf devoted to Dutch literature. A male voice goes on to describe how Mattias has made cuttings from and propagated this cherished ficus, gifting the fledgling plants to friends. The entrancing, multi-vocal narration, with its woodwind accompaniment, conjures—and invites listeners to imagine themselves in—a very personal, enchanting library.

Each chapter likewise conveys compelling details and feelings evoked by the libraries and their queer focus, inviting listeners to wander the full shelves, to kneel down to discover a pamphlet from 1912 behind the glass on the lowest shelf, to gaze out a window onto the street below, to find a folded obituary inside a book, to examine an ex libris bookplate, to read an excerpt of a poem, to discover books arranged in a tiny bathroom, to kiss the pages of a book, to hum in the library and so on. Through these richly layered narratives, Nemer offers listeners the experience, as Foucault once said, of "being places where I am and yet I am not."[9] Echoing Foucault's conceptualization of libraries as portals to elsewhere, Nemer proposes: "By its very nature, a library is multiple, plural, poly. Even though the books are unified in a single space, it seems more fitting to speak in terms of *libraries*."[10] Foucault's theory of heterotopias and heterotopic experiences can be expanded to include the internet, social media and visiting exhibitions online.[11]

Given the present ubiquity of online experiences, we may take for granted Foucault's radical notion of simultaneously experiencing an "elsewhere," but such reflection on his prescient theory illuminates our diverse online experiences in the twenty-first century.

> *There is an old wooden clock mounted to the wall in the hallway, at the threshold to Adrian and Denis's library. If you listen carefully, you will hear another clock: sometimes it is placed in the foyer, sometimes in the sitting room that adjoins the kitchen. Both clocks tell more or less the same time. But the ticking of their tocks are not in sync, and one chimes the hour before the other. They do not tell time, rather they tell times. Listen.*[12]

The weekly pairing of specific audio chapters with floral arrangements, which could be experienced as images online or in person at CUAG, offered an additional entry point and lushness to the audio work. The centrality of flowers in *I Don't Know Where Paradise Is* stems from Nemer's ritual of presenting bouquets to his library hosts when he visits. Flowers have long been agents in Nemer's artistic practice; he deploys their symbolic and aesthetic properties and positions them as witnesses to and participants in human history. Books, like flowers, carry meaning and emotion. Gardens and libraries are likewise developed from cultivation and care and offer spaces of contemplation to nourish the mind and soul.

Flowers can stand in for gardens and allude to an elsewhere "paradise." Perhaps gardens—or libraries—are the elusive paradise named in Nemer's exhibition title, which also elicits the Farsi

The library might overwhelm you by its scale, packed with a dizzying amount of materials, ancestral traces left in the form of books, magazines, pamphlets and journals. But there are gaps, too: missing materials, erased things, feelings and ephemera that do not take archivable form. The spit on your face. The phone number written on a matchbook. The unuttered word. Something that was burned.

But don't despair; these gaps are a material made up of the bonds and barriers that span between us, our ancestors, and those who have yet to appear on the horizon. An admixture of feelings of rage and joy, of ecstasy and abjection, of noises and silences.

And if you listen carefully, if you tune in to these gaps, something emerges.

Listen.

linguistic root of the word "paradise," a walled garden, but that in contemporary meaning, in English, is understood as a dream, a utopia—a placeless place, one that does not exist in reality or that is unattainable, or that we have lost.[13] While Nemer in the use of this exhibition title expresses that the location of paradise eludes him, by citing the ancient Roman philosopher Marcus Tullius Cicero, who wrote, "Si hortum in bibliotheca habes, deerit nihil," he hints that he knows what constitutes paradise: Cicero's words are often translated as, "If you have a garden and a library, you have everything you need."

Nemer's creation of the audio work was grounded in the relationships he built with his hosts and the time he spent in their libraries.[14] In contrast, the floral arrangement component of the exhibition was a collaborative endeavour, realized across the Atlantic, with people Nemer had never met, many of whom had not met one another. The heterotopic potential of online meetings facilitated connections between Nemer and his collaborators, while other aspects of the collaboration occurred independently of him—participants meeting in person, in the flower studio and in the gallery—to dream and realize each week's floral arrangement. Nemer's art practice has long been concerned with fostering queer kinship and connection, and through the heterotopic dimensions of *I Don't Know Where Paradise Is* he opened up possibilities for building queer community, networks, kinship and belonging during a time when the need for connection was keenly felt, amid pandemic lockdowns and physical distancing.

In succession over the course of thirteen weeks, the Ottawa floral respondents—Vincent Edet, Bill Brown and John McKinven (working as a couple), Lydia Collins, Benny Michaud and Sam Loewen—connected with Nemer online and with florist Kat Kosk and CUAG team members, all the while navigating physical distancing and public health measures. These meetings to plan or create the floral arrangements took on added meaning and emotion during a period of restricted social interaction. The respondents shared their ideas for the week's arrangement with Kosk, who then interpreted those ideas. I remember the heightened sense of anticipation of gathering at CUAG on Tuesdays, Kosk and each week's respondent arriving with flowers, various plants, sensuous materials and objects to create the arrangement, which gradually took form in the gallery space through conversation and experimentation.

Because Nemer and the Ottawa participants each created their arrangements in response to the same audio chapter, there was often a discernable affinity between their arrangements. Still, I was struck by the serendipitous rapport between each week's arrangements, and by the inventiveness and unique approach that each of the respondents, with Kosk, brought to the creative process. An attuned floral conversation—a sort of call and response—unfolded between Nemer and his Ottawa-based collaborators.

In response to the inaugural audio chapter, "A Hum in the Library," Vincent Edet created a tall, cascading autumnal bouquet that conjured sombre lushness and decline, which he titled "The Wind Blows on the Dead and the Living." Photographed against the cool green of the walls in CUAG's exhibition space, the pairing with Nemer's spare arrangement of linear, spiralling branches and rose petals, photographed against a dusky crimson-pink wall,

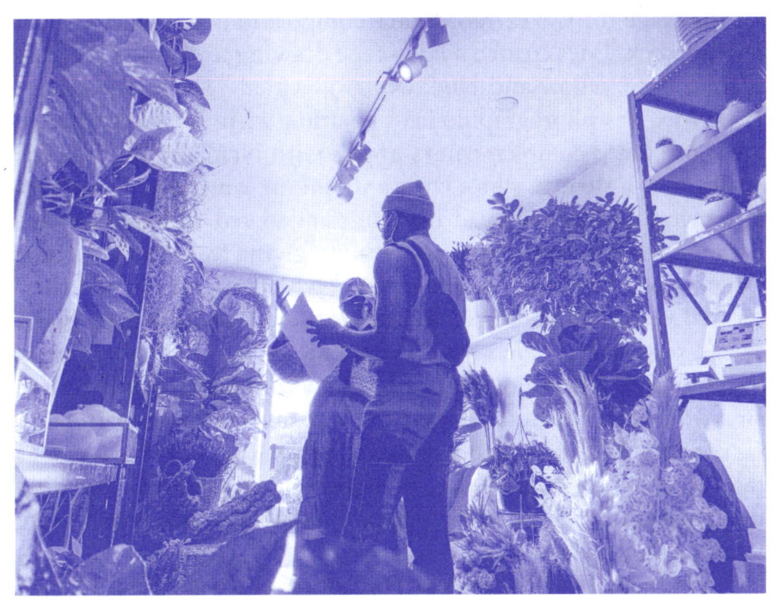

Vincent Edet consults with florist Kat Kosk about materials for his response to Nemer's audio chapter. Photo: Jason Laguerre.

set the stage for the extraordinary compositions to come. The following week, Edet created a landscape drawing in space, with grass plumes dyed yellow and blue, which he titled "The Clouds, They Hide Me." Its photographic juxtaposition with the Paris arrangement produced complementary angles with Nemer's graceful composition of a slender white chrysanthemum, caught and wrapped just below the flower head by a suspended red ribbon threaded through metal script that reads "vrolijk,"giving form to the archaic Dutch word meaning "happy or gay," which appears in the chapter "A Line of Dutch Verse." For week three, "A Capture in Time," Edet's response to Nemer's "A Portrait of Mattias as a Young Faggot" used a tiny Polaroid of a friend who had recently passed away to create a sense of elegy—the bamboo stalks and tumbling vines of red Virginia creeper contrasting with yet echoing Nemer's tall, graceful white gladiolas, their flower-laden stalks extending upwards and downwards from a vase featuring a black-and-white image of Mattias Duyves.

From one week to the next, the notion of what a floral arrangement could be was expanded playfully and poignantly. In week four, Bill Brown and John McKinven's cheeky response "You're Never Safe from Surprises" to the chapter "An Octagonal Mirror" comprised an arrangement of red roses, mullein, pink acetate, a riding crop and a cock ring—the red and pink hues vibrant and seductive. Meanwhile, Nemer slyly anthropomorphized a stunning blue chrysanthemum that appeared to contemplate its reflection in a suspended octagonal mirror.

Being able to go into the gallery, particularly when we had to close periodically due to public health measures, permitted a private experience of each floral arrangement, offering the opportunity to take in scents, textures, perspectives and details not captured by photographs. The arrangements changed subtly from day to day as flowers opened, faded or dropped petals over the course of the week. During the fifth week, when CUAG was closed, I recall the delight of encountering Brown and McKinven's "Sounds of Silence" arrangement alone, when I made a trip in to work. Having only seen the image on Instagram, I was struck and surprised by the ticking of the two clocks, partially obscured by large white hydrangeas, duct tape crisscrossing the face of one clock and electrical tape binding the stems of the leggy chrysanthemums soaring above, which underscored the quiet of the otherwise empty, closed gallery.

Over the weeks that followed, "Books Are Flowers," an arrangement by Lydia Collins, featured paper flowers cut and folded from pages of James Baldwin's *Notes of a Native Son* set among a vivacious mix of flowers, greenery and pine cones. It made for a synergistic pairing with Nemer's plumage-like arrangement placed like a crown on his head. Another week, the chapter "A Urinal" inspired two strikingly minimalist arrangements: Collins created "The Stench of Romance" with roses, craspedia and wire, while Nemer attached chrysanthemum, dahlia and gerbera petals to a metal grid suspended by a length of leather pierced with a pattern of holes.

Meeting over Zoom to prepare for Benny Michaud's response to "A Feather Duster," Kosk joined us from her car en route to forage for plants in the woods and fields. Michaud decided not to use a vase, instead creating "Earth Blanket," with a dramatic woody vine descending over the sides of the plinth from a bed of reindeer moss and palapa. Nemer, who eschewed any "regular" use of a vase in this project, emphasized graceful balance with his arrangement of gaura blossoms, feathers, plastic and leather. For the chapter "Someone Is Weeping in the Library," Nemer suspended a thread with a descent of carnation petals and a single *Ficus elastica* "Variegate" leaf, while Michaud's classy arrangement of amaryllis, baby's breath, orchid and roses was partially obscured as if by a light pink cloud—spray paint on a sheet of acetate suspended from an off-camera bright yellow ladder.

As the weather grew colder and the days shorter, the late-afternoon meetings every Tuesday to create the arrangements became the highlight of the week. I recall the scent of eucalyptus and the allure of amethyst in Sam Loewen's "An Aroma for an Aura," which he created in response to the sensuous chapter "A Bathhouse." This was juxtaposed with Nemer's playful arrangement of accordioned white plastic tubing festooned with verdant viburnum. The following week the chapter "A Postcard of a Still Life" spurred Loewen to create the exuberant "Trouser Snake," which featured a handspun bedsheet rope coiled around a cheery arrangement of pink, peach and yellow. Nemer's corresponding arrangement featured a postcard handmade by his grandmother Rosalie Goodman Namer, and a dramatic single iris tied with ribbon.

On the day the last floral arrangement was created, several CUAG team members, Kosk, Loewen and photographer Olivia Johnston assembled in celebration and remarked on the joy that this exceptional project had brought. Loewen's final arrangement, which he called "The World Will Always Welcome Lovers," featured Icelandic poppies, roses, cedar branches covered in lichen

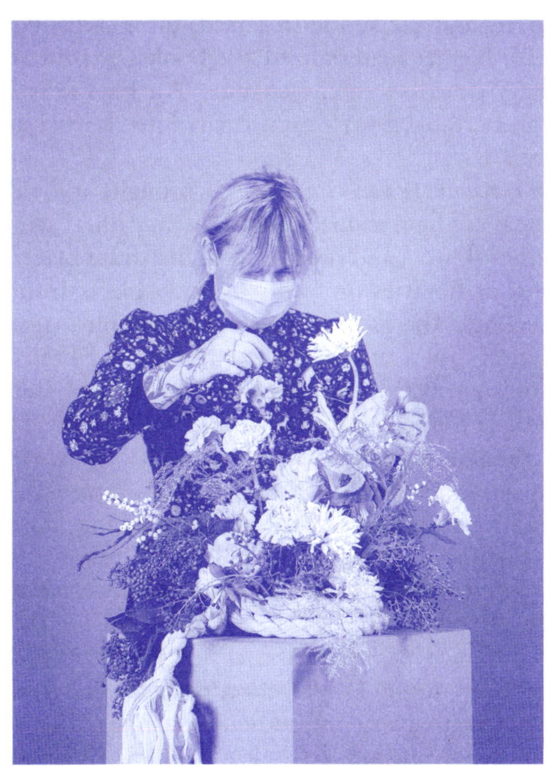

Florist Kat Kosk puts finishing touches on Trouser Snake, *one of Sam Loewen's arrangements at Carleton University Art Gallery. Photo: Olivia Johnston.*

and the Lovers and the World (reversed) tarot cards. For his final arrangement, Nemer materialized the book *Orgasms of Light* he so evocatively describes in the chapter "An Ex Libris Label" on a music stand arranged with mini carnations, leather and a flute mouthpiece.

I Don't Know Where Paradise Is brought individuals into new relational configurations, akin to the way floral arrangements bring together flowers and objects from disparate places, climates and seasons, or libraries unite books and objects from different places and times. The project traversed geography, time and pandemic isolation to activate queer networks and facilitate queer kinship and community.[15] It also extended the sense of discovery and pleasure Nemer found in private queer libraries, among the books' botanical companions and in learning from his hosts.

Benny Nemer's *I Don't Know Where Paradise Is* was for CUAG and its audiences a radical undertaking and beautiful model of collaborative exhibition making. While I propose that Foucault's notion of heterotopic experiences is intrinsic to Nemer's audio work, the realization of this exhibition during the Covid-19 pandemic amplified the character of heterotopic experiences catalyzed by *I Don't Know Where Paradise Is* and resonated in the experiences of participants and audience members dispersed across networks of queer kinship. *I Don't Know Where Paradise Is* creates "elsewhere" spaces—real and imagined—that have long been vital to queer communities and community building. The libraries Nemer visited and shares with us are real spaces, and through his audio work and the archive of floral arrangements, we can visit them anytime. We are invited, in other words, to move with him.

HEATHER ANDERSON

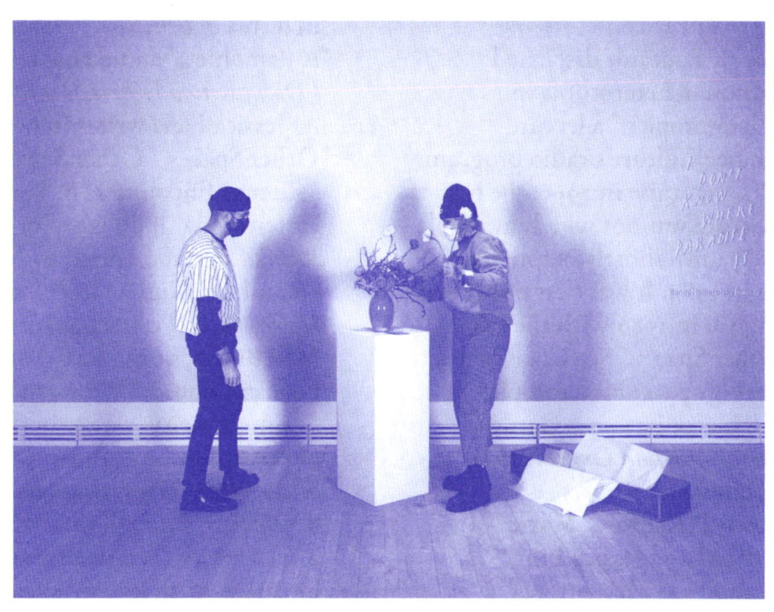

Sam Loewen and Kat Kosk compose
The World Will Always Welcome Lovers *at the gallery.*
Photo: Olivia Johnston.

1 Benny Nemer, "*A Ficus drupacea pubescens*," audio chapter, *I Don't Know Where Paradise Is* (https://where-paradise-is.eu/).

2 Nemer, "A Hum in the Library," audio chapter, ibid.

3 This reimagining was in response to public health and travel restrictions, closures and general uncertainty during summer 2020 and into fall 2020.

4 Although Foucault discussed his notion of heterotopia in "Les Hétérotopies," a lecture for France Culture's radio program Culture française in 1966, the text of this lecture was not widely available publicly until shortly before his death in 1984. It was first published in English in 1986 with the title "Of Other Spaces." See Chris Steyaert, "Queering Space: Heterotopic Life in Derek Jarman's Garden," *Gender, Work and Organization* 17, no 1 (January 2010), 45–68; and Gary P. Radford, Marie L. Radford and Jessica Lingel, "The Library as Heterotopia: Michel Foucault and the Experience of Library Space," *Journal of Documentation* 71, no. 4 (2015): 733–51. Foucault's 1966 lecture can be listened to on YouTube (https://www.youtube.com/watch?v=lxOruDUO4p8).

5 Michel Foucault, "Of Other Spaces," *Diacritics* 16, no. 1 (1986): 22–27, 24.

6 Radford, Radford and Lingel, "The Library as Heteropia," 736

7 Michel Foucault, "Of Other Spaces" cited in Steyaert, "Queering Space," 51.

8 Nemer, "A Line of Dutch Verse," audio chapter, *I Don't Know Where Paradise Is*.

9 Radford, Radford and Lingel, "The Library as Heterotopia," 736.

10 "Can we speak of this collection in the singular, as a library? It seems inaccurate, for it is made up of books and journals and magazines that have arrived from all sorts of other places, all sorts of other libraries. By its very nature, a library is multiple, plural, poly. Even though the books are unified in a single space, it seems more fitting to speak in terms of *libraries*." Nemer, "A Pamphlet," audio chapter, *I Don't Know Where Paradise Is*.

11 As Jessica Fiala writes in her text "Other Spaces / Other Selves: Museum Encounters & Foucault's Heterotopia," published in *The Ruined Archive*, edited by Iain Chambers, Giulia Grechi and Mark Nash (Politecnico di Milano MelaBooks, 2014), 241–262, Foucault noted, "We are in the epoch of simultaneity: we are in the era of juxtaposition ... our experience of the world is less that of a long life developing through time than that of a network that connects points and intersects with its own skein." 244.

12 Nemer, "Two Clocks," audio chapter, *I Don't Know Where Paradise Is*.

13 While "paradise" has come to mean a perfect realm, the word originates in the Farsi word for a walled garden. Merriam-Webster, s.v. "paradise (n.)," https://www.merriam-webster.com/dictionary/paradise.

14 Additionally, Nemer involved many friends in producing the audio work—another aspect of this project that activated a queer network.

15 While the exhibition and its activities have passed, the online content continues to activate queer networks when accessed and shared.

THE TIES THAT BIND: QUEER KINSHIP AS ALTERNATIVE WORLDMAKING IN *PARADISE*

JENNIFER EVANS

I first met Benny Nemer—then based in Berlin—at the Alberta College of Art and Design in Calgary, Alberta, in the winter of 2011, an odd place for an art exhibition and conference on the legacy of sexology and the German gay rights movement. *PopSex!* was inspired by an earlier exhibition at Berlin's Charité Hospital commemorating the burning of books from Magnus Hirschfeld's Institute for Sexual Research. Curated by Rainer Herrn, Annette Timm and Michael Taylor, *PopSex!* marked the beginning of a series of transatlantic collaborations among the three friends, who would go on to produce the *TransTrans* exhibition, tracing the migration of ideas and research around transsexual/transgender life and science.[1] It was itself an example of the networks and pathways that link queer and trans art, science and ideas across the Atlantic, in elaborate aesthetic and museological perambulations. It also was the beginning of conversations between Benny and me on the transformative potential of the illicit in queer aesthetic modes of representing the past.[2]

It was in cold Calgary, in other words, that Benny and I discovered we shared the warmth of kinship, an emotional and intellectual linking of spirit and mind around our shared curiosity for queer lives and loves past and present. Over several years, we would nurture this kinship in our own way, in our separate but related registers.[3] I would write articles about Benny's art practice, and he would include me in various events that served as staging grounds for his ideas around sound, movement, embodiment and gesture that ultimately culminated in the CUAG exhibition *I Don't Know Where Paradise Is* (*Paradise* for short). We brought our two approaches together in a blended, multi-modal, performative keynote for a gender conference in Gothenburg, Sweden, where we presented to the audience the power of empathic listening in opening pathways into the erotohistory of queer and trans elders. Benny's sound stories and the aural experience of listening, whether alone or in a group, intrigued me for the way they serve as portals. I was drawn to how he used the affective dimension of sound to de-normalize the familiar, creating lush sensory encounters that allow us to connect with, reimagine and understand anew everyday ambiences of experience in novel and exploratory ways. These aural ecologies, how each of us intervenes in the sonic landscape as we make our way through the shuffled middle chapters of the *I Don't Know Where Paradise Is* audio guide, allow us to imagine along with the narrators what we find there, creating conditions of commonality amidst our subjective differences. Benny's curation of these sonic experiences builds bonds of kinship with the past. It works against temporalities of pain and loss, and brings into view what Elizabeth Freeman calls "the value of surprise, of pleasurable interruptions and momentary fulfillments from elsewhere, other times."[4] Although vastly different interlocutors, Benny and I are both interested in the mediational role of technology and the aesthetic sensibilities that help build these ties that bind us, and how they might serve to connect us all to queer history, in a way that not only honours but also celebrates our different points of entry and ways of working through.

Although the *Paradise* project began with the prospect of creating an audio guide that connected the library collections of queer elders, it quickly evolved into the story of erotic perambulations themselves, of curiosity, cruising, intellectual and metaphysical coming together within the gendered expectations, orientations

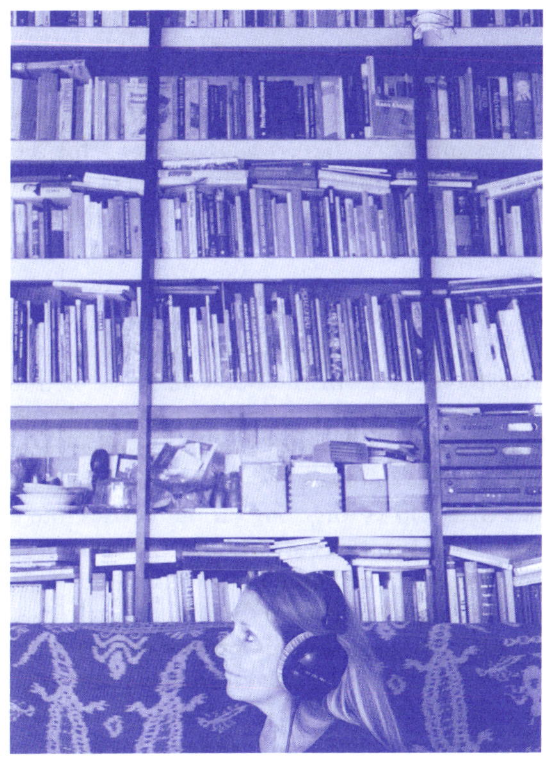

Jennifer Evans listens to a first draft of Nemer's audio guide as part of a research action in the Amsterdam home of Gert Hekma and Mattias Duyves in 2017. Photo: Benny Nemer.

and performances of everyday life. Moving through and beyond texts, encountering objects, conjuring lifeworlds and new as well as old ways of being in the world as friends, admirers and as lovers imagining otherwise, as Saidiya Hartman famously wrote in *Wayward Lives, Beautiful Experiments* (2019). This set of stories evocatively rendered, in other words, became a blueprint for a kind of kinship that moves beyond the heteronormative framework of family to include bonds of emotional and sometimes physical intimacy, rituals of togetherness, shared confessions and symbols, common associations, love, lust and ideas. It is queer worldmaking, *tout court*. Using voice, song, touch, imagination, reading and the books and material items found in the home libraries of these scholar/ancestors, *Paradise* compels listeners to move with the narrators backwards and forwards through time, conjuring, reconstructing and creating anew the emotional, social, intellectual and sometimes sexual bonds that help us forge our various entries into the history, present and possible futurities of 2SLGBTQ+ communities.

The contents of these home libraries are not the sole focus—and indeed, among the libraries Benny researched and visited, some that lent inspiration to this project are no longer even in existence, as in the case of the one created by photographer Hervé Guibert, who succumbed to AIDS at the age of thirty-six. His books and ephemera, boxed and stored in Paris, documented through sketches and reminiscences of what once was, inspired Benny to think of ways one might represent the no longer physically tangible. Although Guibert's library is not a featured chapter in *Paradise*, this sentiment of life, love and loss plays a tangible part in its conceptualization. Indeed it is what queer libraries and their

Asked about the relationship between the library and the garden, Mattias responds that books are flowers and flowers are books. But what exactly does that mean? That each flower tells a story? That the pages of a book are as precious as the fragile petals of a peony? Adrian and Denis's library is wall-papered with a pattern of branches, acorns, birds and butterflies, giving readers the impression of sitting in an enchanted forest. Plants with long histories climb the bookshelves and hang from the staircases of Tom's library, and his roof terrace is surrounded by box elder trees. So maybe there is some relationship between flowers and books, some kinship or simultaneity that our hosts understand.

holdings open up and enable, whether as a literal archive of past lives or of what Ann Cvetkovich has called an archive of feeling, a real or imagined repository of shifting thoughts, sentiments, memories and emotions that make up what it means to enter into queer relation to the past.[5] These libraries tell their own stories of queerness, sometimes as identity but also, in Carolyn Dinshaw's sense, as a kind of slippage between norms and lack of fit.[6] By providing us with points of orientation, real or imagined, Benny's sound pieces entreat their listeners to respond on impulse and conjure for themselves, through their senses, the shape and contours of these queer ecologies.[7] In privileging the sense of listening and sound as subjectivity's vector, the guide narrates an encounter with queerness as a polyvalent "space of entrances, exits, unsystematized lines of acquaintance, projecting horizons, typifying examples, alternate routes, blockages, [and] incommensurate geographies."[8] The world thus revealed relationally is a series of encounters between our own bodies in the present and the intimacies of the past given form through story and voice. Just as it materializes a whiff of what once was, there is always a slant, an untidy affordance that disrupts the possibility of scripted conventions and heteronormative alignments.[9] That slant is the sumptuousness of queer desire.

Each chapter of *Paradise* unfolds in a narrative read by different voices with different cadences, and is focused around an object, a passage in a book or several books in a bathroom, a clock, a plant and a mirror, creating what the artist refers to as "a touch across time." This way of evoking pastness through objects and story links the history of bathrooms and urinals and bathhouses to reading, cruising and collecting as part of the search for queer selfhood in the present. But it is not about eliding time and collapsing difference. It is a search for sameness while recognizing essential differences, one that counters simple "mimetic identification with the past or blanket alteritism" to make plain the "never-perfect aspect of identification" with "incommensurate lives and phenomena."[10]

This approach holds great power. For those typically written out of history, memory is "a valuable historical resource, and ephemeral and personal collections of objects stand alongside the documents of the dominant culture in order to offer alternative modes of knowledge."[11] Indeed, this "will to remember," whether in history writing or in building community archives, has played a guiding role in 2SLGBTQI+ consciousness during these last decades.[12] As Heather Love says in *Feeling Backward*, knowledge of "the losses of the past motivate us and give meaning to our current experience." It galvanizes a sense of imperative to continue fighting for rights and representation. Because successes can always be unmade, Love argues, "we are bound to memorialize" losses. Remembering the past as tragedy acts as a call to arms against present-day mistreatment, creating a shared struggle as a stand-in for lineage, an origin story, in the quest to "overcome that past, to escape its legacy" and never go back."[13] But pinned to this notion of the past as trauma are two things countered in Benny's project: a nostalgia for a history told solely through suffering and the use of this narrative in stabilizing a vision of the present as a process of continual overcoming.

Through circuitous routes, *Paradise* lays this foundation for a new kind of history, one that proposes a relational, sensorially driven mode of making and communicating diverse pasts and with them new futures. Benny's use of voice, storytelling, gesture,

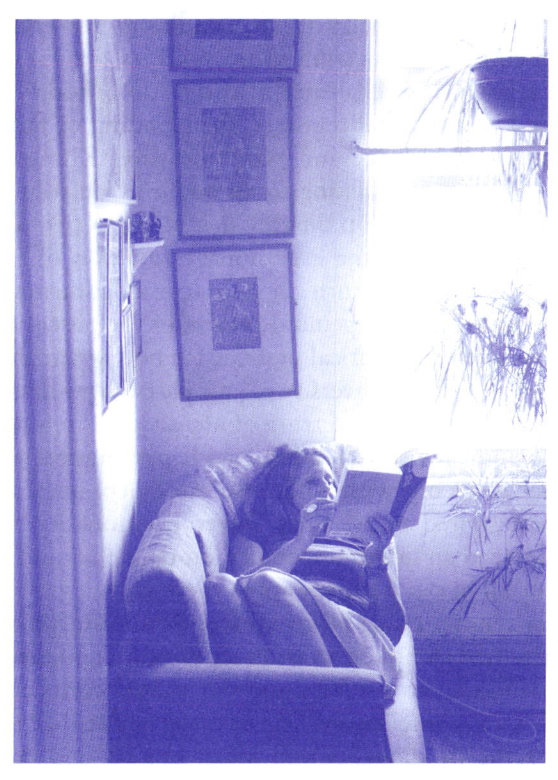

Jennifer Evans follows a navigational score by Nemer as part of a research action in the Montreal home of Tom Waugh in 2018. Photo: Benny Nemer.

movement and sound helps create conditions for empathic listening, widening the spectrum of possibilities for ways to think about the relationship of history to the world of today. This mix of aesthetic and historical registers, the blending of fact with fiction, stresses multivalence and possibility over a singular narrative truth. The act of listening to an audio guide outside of the gallery or museum space promotes shared subjective commensurabilities that challenge the exclusionary function of traditional museum displays, which turn on objective, documentary claims while often reflecting a hegemonic vision of the past. In this way, Benny offers a queer historical practice for how we might (re)present and engage with the diversity of past pasts, regardless of where we are positioned on the spectrum of identity. His multi-sensorial approach conjures "new relations... with past figures who elude resemblance to us but with whom we can be connected partially by virtue of shared marginality, queer positionality."[14] Placing emphasis instead on multitemporality, on the nodes and networks that bind us all in our unique ways to these various pasts and presents, Benny's audio guide offers up a critical nostalgia instead of a redemptive one alongside an embrace of new contemporary and future possibilities, focused around our shared connectedness to queer ancestors, whose lessons help us navigate the road ahead.

The traffic in thoughts and ideas, objects and collectables, however, is porous. It replicates our multiple affiliations while pointing at the limits of boundaries of identity. Benny's evocations wrestle with this simultaneity, at once honouring the rarified and at times exclusionary literary and visual iconographies of cruising, intergenerational sex, race and beauty, while opening up moments of reflection around the very politics of visibility itself, including the eroticization of a whole host of others. This is not homo-nostalgia, as Gloria Wekker rightfully calls out in *White Innocence*; it is an aesthetic appeal for a more embodied, intersectional memory.[15]

But the ties that bind here go beyond what is found in the libraries themselves and the connections between the books and their authors, readers, owners and users. It is also found in what is not represented in the library. As Benny says in the opening sequence of the audio guide, drawing on the work of Black studies visual culture scholar Tina Campt, it is the soft hum of the not yet known or unrepresentable pushing its way back into our frame.[16] Or as Benny puts it in the opening chapter, "A vibration comes from the library: a hum. Is it the hum of the books? The murmur of characters and diagrams and photographs tightly pressed between pages, rubbing up against each other? Is it the hum of the things that for one reason or another did not find their ways into the library, humming, calling out for a reader?" These traces of lost, subterranean lives materialize in our ears and minds through the encounters offered up to us through ambulatory, improvisational and scripted paths into and through these libraries, highlighting the recursive power that dwells in "the open mesh of possibilities, gaps, overlaps, dissonances and resonances, lapses and excesses of meaning" that make up queer worldmaking.[17] Just as it is impossible to know the entirety of the contents of the library, so too is it impossible to reproduce the complexity of queer kinship. If it is to be found, it is in the hum that holds out the ever-present promise of possibility, of connection across time, of imagining the queer past anew, for all of its kin.[18]

JENNIFER EVANS

1 The exhibition *TransTrans: Transatlantic Transgender Histories* was held in 2016. See Alex Bakker et al., *Others of My Kind: Transatlantic Transgender Histories* (Calgary: University of Calgary Press, 2020).
2 Michael Taylor and Annette F. Timm, "Sex on Display: Sexual Science and the Exhibition *PopSex!*," in Peter M. McIsaac and Gabriele Mueller, *Exhibiting the German Past: Museums, Film, and Musealization* (Toronto: University of Toronto Press, 2015).
3 Bakker et al., *Others of My Kind*.
4 Elizabeth Freeman, "Theorizing Queer Temporalities: A Roundtable Discussion," *GLQ* 13, nos. 2–3 (2007): 59.
5 Ann Cvetkovich, *An Archive of Feeling: Sexuality, and Lesbian Public Cultures* (Durham, NC: Duke University Press, 2003).
6 Carolyn Dinshaw, *Getting Medieval: Sexualities and Communities, Pre- and Postmodern*, Series Q (Durham, NC: Duke University Press, 1999), 39.
7 Sara Ahmed, *Queer Phenomenology: Orientations, Objects, Others* (Durham, NC: Duke University Press, 2006).
8 Lauren Berlant and Michael Warner, "Sex in Public," in *Publics and Counterpublics*, by Michael Warner (New York: Zone Books, 2005), 198.
9 Judith Halberstam, *In a Queer Time and Place: Transgender Bodies, Subcultural Lives*, Sexual Culture Series (New York: New York University Press, 2005), 9.
10 Dinshaw, *Getting Medieval*, 21.
11 Cvetkovich, *An Archive of Feeling*, 8.
12 Joan Nestle, "The Will to Remember: The Lesbian Herstory Archives of New York," *Feminist Review* 34, no. 1 (1 March 1990): 86–94, https://doi.org/10.1057/fr.1990.12.
13 Heather Love, *Feeling Backward: Loss and the Politics of Queer History* (Cambridge, MA: Harvard University Press, 2009), 1.
14 Dinshaw, *Getting Medieval*, 21.
15 Gloria Wekker, *White Innocence: Paradoxes of Colonialism and Race* (Durham, NC: Duke University Press, 2016).
16 Tina Campt, *Listening to Images* (Durham, NC: Duke University Press, 2017).
17 Eve Kosofsky Sedgwick, "Queer and Now," in *Tendencies*, Series Q (New York: Routledge, 1994), 8.
18 Jennifer V. Evans, *The Queer Art of History: Queer Kinship after Fascism* (Durham, NC: Duke University Press, 2023).

THE SOUND OF BOOKS AND FLOWERS: QUEERING THE AUDIO GUIDE

ANN CVETKOVICH

Despite the challenges posed by the Covid-19 pandemic, I was able to visit the Carleton University Art Gallery to see two of the thirteen floral arrangements created in Ottawa for *I Don't Know Where Paradise Is*. It felt important to see the arrangements in person, like a visit to one of the libraries that inspired the exhibition or a pilgrimage to an icon or an altar in a church, to honour the material presence of the live flowers and show up for an exhibition whose conditions were dramatically transformed by the pandemic. And the two arrangements that I saw—created by Vincent Edet in response to Benny Nemer's audio chapter "A Portrait of Mattias as a Young Faggot," and by Sam Loewen in response to "A Bathhouse"—were indeed beautiful, with their combinations of living plants and charged objects: a vine with dried autumn leaves and a Polaroid photograph pinned to two stalks of bamboo, a nest of cedar sprigs and baby eucalyptus pierced with steel grass perched on top of a clear glass vessel housing an amethyst crystal, set against the cool green background of the wall and plinth on which they stood.

I also appreciated that CUAG had created space to hang out and listen to the audio work that is the foundation for the show, although given the impossibility of large gatherings, the six chairs arranged in the empty gallery seemed like wishful fantasy or forbidden pleasure. On one of my visits, though, I met with Cara Tierney, co-curator with Anna Shah Hoque of the other exhibition in the space, *To Be Continued: Troubling the Queer Archive*, a wonderful counterpart to Benny Nemer's show that filled the galleries with the textures and colours of Ed Kwan's China Doll costumes, Barry Ace's bandoliers, Howard Adler's meme installation and Ashley Grenstone's book manuscript ephemera, to name a few. Sitting in the chairs next to the floral arrangement, masked and two metres apart, felt like a semblance of the queer sociality that the pandemic has taken from us and that *I Don't Know Where Paradise Is* seeks to conjure.

I Don't Know Where Paradise Is was designed to function independently of the gallery's unpredictable Covid-19 schedule. The audio work was available as a web-based app, and the weekly floral arrangements took on a life of their own online as photographic diptychs pairing arrangements made by Nemer in his Paris studio with those of Ottawa-Gatineau queers working in tandem with florist Kat Kosk. Effecting an otherwise impossible co-presence, the arrangements inspired by Nemer's audio chapters spoke to one another across time, space and media—in assemblages of objects and living plants that transitioned from material presence to electronic image. Although by nature a floral arrangement is alive and ephemeral, as with many icons both sacred and secular, their photographic reproductions also carried the aura of the animate, and the constellation of organic and inorganic materials in each arrangement was further extended by the juxtaposition of each pair. In viewing them alongside Nemer's homage to books and libraries in the audio chapters, I was reminded of my own interest in what I call the "bibliographic altar"—arrangements of books and artifacts that make thinking sensory and material and can create an "archive of feelings." Flowers and other forms of what archivists and natural historians might call "botanical specimens" often find their ways onto such altars in both live and preserved states as material embodiments or remnants of memories and ephemeral

There is a rather magical looking octagonal mirror mounted to the wall by the main entrance, just across from the rotating shelves. The surface of the mirror is slightly warped, as though the glass shivered with pleasure while it was being silvered. If you stand to the right or left and gaze into the mirror – sideways – you will catch a glimpse of the infinity of books stacked in the library.

There are so many words in the library, yet a lack of language to express one's feelings and desires is a common human condition. Looking through the mirror, at the other library, one wonders if the words you are looking for are in *those* books. Or in other things in the mirror: the window that opens onto the canal, the bouquet of last-weeks delphiniums and aspedistra leaves, the reflection of your shoulder.

moments. So I felt very much at home with Nemer's approach to the floral arrangements, as well as with the affective relations he fosters with and between books and flowers, libraries and gardens. The exhibition's flexibility across media and adaptation to pandemic conditions also worked because the audio piece at the heart of the project, *I Don't Know Where Paradise Is*, can be experienced anywhere. Like Nemer, I've always been ambivalent about museum audio guides because they can be a bad version of the wall labels and overload viewers with information that prevents them from experiencing the displays for themselves. They are also part of a history of problematic colonial and patriarchal framing, including failures to mention queer histories or to attend to ghostly presences and absences. The audio guide often controls where you stand and what's deemed important, and the steady soundtrack can prevent you from hearing yourself think. When in a museum, I've taken to resisting the captivity of the audio guide by strolling at leisure while listening, sometimes watching the work being discussed from the other side of the room, or going somewhere else entirely, absorbing the information in a more sensory or kinesthetic way by moving through space.

I'm delighted that Nemer's audio work frees us to become flâneurs who can roam anywhere, while also inviting us to be in the libraries he conjures. Each audio chapter activates his practice as a sound artist who resists the typical bland pedagogical authority of the audio guide in favour of sound collages that combine different voices, music and sounds. One of my best experiences of *I Don't Know Where Paradise Is* was listening to the audio segments on a late summer day during the pandemic, when listening to podcasts has connected me to other places and voices in the absence of social contact. While walking in the tall grasses under the powerlines in my neighbourhood, I could be transported to the library of Gert Hekma and Mattias Duyves in Amsterdam or a bathhouse in Montreal through the ekphrastic power of Nemer's descriptions of books and other objects. Six months later, I visited the same audio versions of objects and spaces during winter, amid snow and naked trees. Sometimes now when I walk those paths, one of Nemer's libraries will come to me.

Like many queer artists working in archives and museums, Nemer offers a queer take on conventional genres, using the audio guide as a way to conjure what is not there, allowing us to visit very personal queer libraries that are not typically accessible to the public, simply through an experience of sound collage that includes multiple voices as well as music and humming. Although every listening experience is different, owing to the app's shuffling of the segments, they all begin with "A Hum in the Library," which prepares us for a personal experience and a set of encounters that aren't organized as authoritative knowledge. The listener is invited to tune in to what is not there, as well as to what is there, to remember the gaps and absences, and to experience the affective life of the books and objects in the library as coming through the vibration of the hum as much as through spoken words and text.

Through sound, Nemer takes us to the libraries of noted gay male activists and intellectuals who have accumulated vast collections as part of their work—we travel to the homes and bookshelves of Gert Hekma and Mattias Duyves in Amsterdam, Adrian Rifkin in London, René Schérer in Paris and Tom Waugh in Montreal.

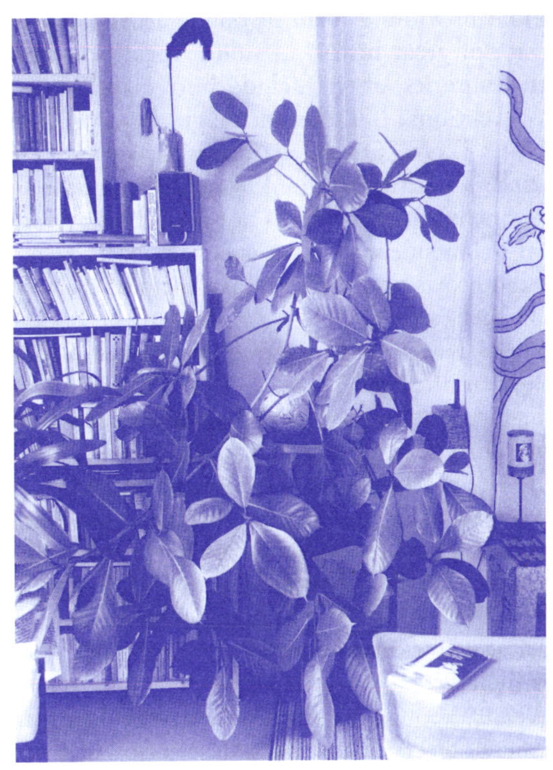

A plant in the library of Gert Hekma and Mattias Duyves mentioned in "A Ficus drupacea pubescens," one of the chapters of I Don't Know Where Paradise Is. *Photo: Benny Nemer.*

Nemer's audio provides a form of public access to private collections that are of great historical value. These very personal and idiosyncratic libraries often include books and collections not found in conventional libraries, although that is changing as the value of these 2SLGBTQ+ collections is recognized and such private collections are being acquired by public institutions. Like the book collectors he visits, Nemer is not just a bibliophile but also a bibliosexual—someone who experiences a book as akin to a sexual encounter and browsing the library as a form of cruising, whether walking the shelves or finding a volume on the back of a toilet. Opening a book is a form of encounter with a person, or a feeling—an act of love or affective intimacy. And the audio chapters also describe the forms of hospitality and queer sociality that his hosts have fostered through their homes and their books.

And it's not just books. While some of the audio chapters are focused on books, others are focused on objects—a mirror, a clock, a photograph, a sign on the wall. Nemer is attuned to the library as an archive of feelings that encompasses not just books but also the space itself and the things in it as material expressions or repositories of queer affective experience. In some cases, the objects in his audio work include text or overlap with the books, such as "A Line of Dutch Verse," about a sign from the gay bookstore Vrolijk. By including these objects in the audio description of these personal libraries, Nemer reminds us that the books are located in spaces, often intimate and domestic ones, and that his visits to these libraries include a keen awareness of his surroundings.

The audio chapters transform objects into a listening experience through careful descriptions of the artifacts, conjuring them

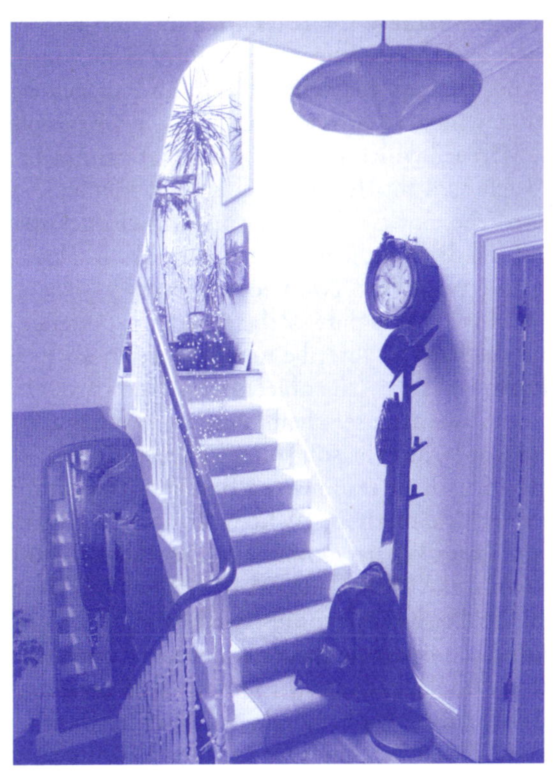

One of two clocks in the London home of Adrian Rifkin and Denis Echard mentioned in the audio chapter "Two Clocks." Photo: Benny Nemer.

for us. However, because the texts are aural and not written, the readers' voices and the accompanying sounds also evoke the hushed reverence and feelings that the objects and spaces evoke. They speak to that which is beyond words—as, for example, in "The Octagonal Mirror," which reflects on all that cannot be expressed in words, such as a touch on the shoulder. Nemer's attunement to sound—to the clocks whose ticking and chimes speak to one another and tell different kinds of time (in "Two Clocks"), to choral singing and music (in "Two Clock Towers")—is a reminder of the sound archive that is part of the sensory experience of a space, and that can be hard to describe in words and hard to archive. By various means, we "hear" the objects displayed through the audio chapters, even if we can't see them. And in "Someone Is Weeping," there are no words, just the soft sound of weeping (not crying) and ethereal music, as if in response to Barthes's important question for affective archival method, "Who will write the history of tears?"

I Don't Know Where Paradise Is also takes us to places outside and beyond the library, such as the urinal and the bathhouse, which are central to any queer affective history. Although libraries can certainly become erotic spaces and sites of cruising, especially when there are books in the bathroom or on the nightstand, these other kinds of spaces of ephemeral encounter need to be preserved somehow, and the audio chapter is a means to bring them into the space of exhibition alongside the library. Nemer describes the urinal as an archive of piss (and sex) that also finds its way into the library and into history through the many books about its importance as a site of cruising. The bathhouse in which Tom Waugh holds meetings for gay male students in an old-school version of

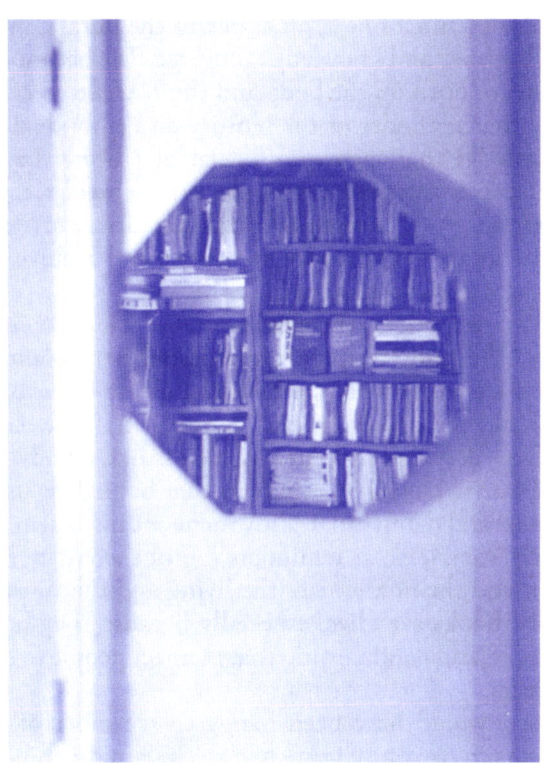

Books in the library of Gert Hekma and Mattias Duyves are reflected in the mirror referred to in the audio chapter "An Octagonal Mirror." Photo: Benny Nemer.

Greek pedagogy functions as an annex to the library and another site where both sex and knowledge converge. The bathhouse whose heat and steam open up the body and the senses to receive knowledge is another reminder of the sensory and embodied nature of queer knowledge that the audio format of *I Don't Know Where Paradise Is* also enables by making the ears a site of reception and encouraging the body to comport itself in a variety of ways. Going beyond the library is critical for the ephemeral archive of feeling and sensations that is central to queer history.

Flowers and books are close kin in *I Don't Know Where Paradise Is*. The audio chapters often describe the plants that are in the libraries along with the books, and in "A *Ficus drupacea pubescens*," Nemer makes explicit connections between gardens and libraries: "A house without a garden is like a body without a soul." "A Feather Duster" reminds us that books are also organic matter—dust and damp can destroy them or cause them to decay—but, as such, they serve as reminders too of the entanglements of the human and the nonhuman, the living and the so-called dead. Like plants, books are alive, especially because they both create networks of relation and kinship that connect people to each other and to objects.

While I would have been happy to see more of the floral arrangements in person (CUAG had to close mid-exhibition), one of the best ways to experience them was online—not only in the beautiful diptychs created between Ottawa and Paris each week, but also in the cumulative online grid display on CUAG's website that turns them into a series, and an archive of the collective process generated by the weekly collaborations. Even if we can't see all the details of each arrangement or experience their scents, we can see an array of shapes and colours, including the shifting background colours, all of which contribute to an electronic version of the abundance that even a simple bouquet of flowers can provide. The collection of images—like a collection of books—stands as the record of a serial practice that has been, for this viewer, something of a lifeline in this time of uncertainty.

Producing something each week, and in tandem with others, is a way of saying I'm still alive—literally so, given the live presence of the floral arrangements. This model for a practice of memorial and reflection is valuable in this moment when so many have died while we have had no time or space for sharing grief. The relay across media —from the libraries to Nemer's descriptive text, to its audio performance, to collaborative floral arrangements and then to photographs to be viewed online—makes the exhibition highly portable, and nimble enough to conjure multiple feelings as well as a kind of sociality of feelings. To have been able to take a moment to contemplate these arrangements whether in person or online has been a balm. And the accumulated record will perhaps offer testimony that we have persisted in the face of the challenges of this pandemic time.

ANN CVETKOVICH

IN THE SPACES OF BIBLIOSEXUALITY: THE LIBRARY AS EXTRAVAGANT GESTURE AND QUEER UTOPIA

JOHN POTVIN

Libraries are odd places. The dust they contain is a nightmare for those suffering from allergies. They are the spaces that physically, culturally, symbolically and metaphorically house knowledge, both past and present, with the permissive soupçon of an unknown future. With all the wisdom they contain, libraries have also been seen as threatening, for they test the limits of the relationship between knowledge and power. Nevertheless, the books they hold are things of beauty not exclusively for the words that populate their pages, but also for the labour and love involved in the making of the physical object. Newer glossy, slick editions over which the hand glides quickly have their own sensual experience as do those tomes fortunate enough to be bound in leather, providing, as artist Benny Nemer describes, "an orgy of bookbinding frottage," in his audio work exploring the private libraries of elder gay scholars, *I Don't Know Where Paradise Is*. Libraries are spaces where touch and sight are bound in a holy and seemingly illicit union. Holding a book in my hand, I am allowed—nay expected—to be looking at its pages, yet, my eyes are also drawn elsewhere: to other books, to personal objects or to other bodies populating the space. Libraries are spaces of distraction and also of deep focus and contemplation, of abandoned meandering. They are spaces where time is used wisely and squandered freely. They invite that delightful childhood pastime of daydreaming that is often lost with the onset of adulthood and responsibility. Libraries are imposingly organized and yet through their geometric structure and ordering system they provide the potential for illicit activity. Libraries house many secrets...

Scholars have largely tended to focus on the content of libraries; they rarely think about their ephemerality, or the performances and experiences also housed within these spaces. This is not entirely surprising for as queer theorist José Esteban Muñoz reminds us, "[w]ork that attempts to index the anecdotal, the performative, or the ephemeral as proof is often undermined by the academy's officiating structures."[1] However, these traces are the very thing that Benny Nemer attempts to capture, explore and celebrate in his compelling exhibition for Carleton University Art Gallery (CUAG), *I Don't Know Where Paradise Is,* featuring his eponymous audio work. In the harsh reality that the Covid-19 pandemic has wrought, the exhibition morphed to focus on Nemer's audio guide and explore what a queer approach to the audio guide can do or be. Nemer queries the steadfast subject-object relationship, compelling the listener to recall their own embodiment, memories and experiences by making meaning through desire and eroticism. This is a rather strange proposition; that is, embodiment is centered around a dislocated act of solitary listening in the comfort of one's own home, in the gallery, on a walk or perhaps even in one's own library. Yet, Nemer's evocative and soothing voice allows a comfort all its own, a safety to explore the four international private, personal libraries[2] that comprise the exhibition's physical premise. According to the audio guide, the visitor—or perhaps more aptly, the interloper—is guided through a series of private libraries. Nemer began his research in the library of Gert Hekma and Mattias Duyves's home in Amsterdam and enlarged his scope to include the libraries of Hervé Guibert (Paris), Matthias Herrmann (Vienna), Adrian Rifkin (London), René Schérer (Paris) and

The plant drapes its tentacles across the bookshelf, groping its own selection of books with its curved yellow-green fingers. It has more hands and perhaps more minds than we do, so it can simultaneously read "The Same-Sex Kamasutra," "Scatology," and "The Myth of the Mannish Lesbian." Does the plant read the books, or does it know some other mode of edification? Are the plants of the library nourished by more than just water and sunlight? Surely they absorb book molecules, the library dust, as well as the traces of our touches as our fingers leaf the pages. Are the books and their readers part of the plant's bloodstream? Where is the separation?

Thomas Waugh (Montreal). These extensive libraries are not simply the product of collecting, but the material remnants of decades devoted to scholarship.

The audio guide is comprised of twenty-five discrete chapters, yet the interloper is only privy to six or so in one visit, impelling one to make many visits.[3] This act of repetition, however, is rewarded by continuous and different experiences of these spaces and even adjacent spaces that connect in myriad ways to the four personal libraries that became the focus of Nemer's project. Each chapter promises to only provide fragments, notes, series of studies, expression of movements. Indeed, through these aural tidbits, the audio guide offers up a generative evocation of the ways in which archives are themselves incomplete, fragmentary and inhospitable to those searching out the histories and narratives of queer identities. Although Nemer takes his cues and inspiration from the notion of the archive as source of meaning and knowledge, thankfully the spaces he works with and evokes through the exhibition are firmly rooted in the present moment, allowing for an entire repository of embodied knowledge to unfold—the very material that fuels the audio guide.

Although pandemic restrictions meant that CUAG was accessible to the museum-goer for only a few short weeks, the randomly selected chapters in the audio guide's conceptualization nevertheless disrupted the conventional sequencing of the white cube gallery that dominates our experience of art museums. Rather, *I Don't Know Where Paradise Is* offers a series of ever-changing encounters with libraries that dissuades us from the notion of ever really "knowing" them in their entirety. In fact, Nemer notes how all his hosts are aware of their incomplete knowledge of their own libraries. Rather than linear or chronological, Nemer offers a queer temporality purposefully in opposition to what Elizabeth Freeman defines as chrononormativity, which is the way time is harnessed "to organise individual human bodies toward maximum productivity." Chrononormativity is the clear product of the intersecting histories of industrial capitalism and the birth of the sexual deviant, the effects of which are "teleological schemes of events or strategies for living such as marriage, accumulation of health and wealth for the future, reproduction, childrearing, and death and its attendant rituals."[4] In the chapter "Two Clocks" Nemer narrates how two clocks in Adrian Rifkin's library "do not tell time, rather they tell times... the rhythm of the library's frottage of temporalities." Through Nemer's atemporal queer audio guide, the interloper's body moves virtually from space to space, and where or when one finds oneself is not always clear, engendering novel and unexpected connections through space and time. For Nemer, what connects these chapters are those gaps and feelings, those things absent, inadmissible, from the public archive. One is therefore expected to *feel* one's way through the labyrinth of the library.

So much of the extant scholarship and artistic initiatives exploring queer experiences, expressions and interventions have largely revolved within the public sphere. This is not an entirely surprising reality given how public spaces (parks, urinals, etc.) were if not a, then *the* primary facilitator of same-sex sexual encounter, particularly among men throughout the nineteenth and twentieth centuries. In more recent years, scholars have increasingly turned their attention to the private domestic realm.[5] The so-called ideal divide marking the gendered division between the feminized domestic realm and the masculinist public domain has also been perceived, erroneously, as a concern around safety—the domestic purportedly providing a safe haven. However, with increased awareness, intolerance of and public discourses around sexual violence at home or familial intolerance of queer or trans children, the domestic sphere is understood to be as precarious and inhospitable a site as the city or town. The rules, beliefs, stereotypes and structures buttressing the sanctity and promise of domestic bliss have given way to a whole new assortment of re-imaginings of kinship and domestic intimacy.

Herein lies the creative intervention that Nemer provides. His project fits within a growing body of creative work that sets out to challenge what the domestic interior is or should be through a queer framing. Of note is Afrikaner textile artist Pierre le Riche's *The Rainbow Room* (2012), which explores the complicated histories of discrimination, masculinity, sexuality and gay identity in a post-Apartheid South Africa. Also of note here is the work of the internationally renowned duo Michael Elmgreen and Ingar Dragset whose specially commissioned *Tomorrow* (2013–14), staged at the Victoria and Albert Museum in London, and its sequel, *Past Tomorrow* (2015), at Galerie Perrotin in New York, set out to reclaim furniture and space toward decidedly queer ends.[6]

The Hum

The surprising heart, sound and feeling of Nemer's audio guide is humming. Introduced in the first chapter, "A Hum in the Library," the hum emerges from the space of the library. It is central to the embodiment Nemer is attempting to engender. He poetically describes the meanings of the hum:

> A vibration comes from the library: a hum. Is it the hum of the books? The murmur of characters and diagrams and photographs pressed tightly between pages, rubbing up against each other? Is it the hum of all the things that for one reason or another did not find their ways into the library, humming, calling out for a reader?
> It is the hum that staves off the ache of loneliness—
> The hum that soothes the smarting pain of rejection—
> The hum of wondering when you'll see him again—
> The low hum in your pelvis—
> The hum after—[7]

Humming is so often transgressive, especially in a library, which, like a gallery, tacitly and overtly enforces protocols of decorum and silence. But in a personal library? Humming? The hums in the audio guide become a meditative release within the sanctuary of the personal cum public space of the library. Humming moves from embodied experience, expression and vibration to a form of intimacy. Harnessed by Nemer, humming becomes a sensory conduit, a sexual liberation, a spatial grounding, an expression of desire itself. The hum as invocation that inhabits the mesmerizing audio guide sits within a liminal space between noise and silence, between meditation and the incessant hum of the technologies that inhabit our homes and dominate our public lives.

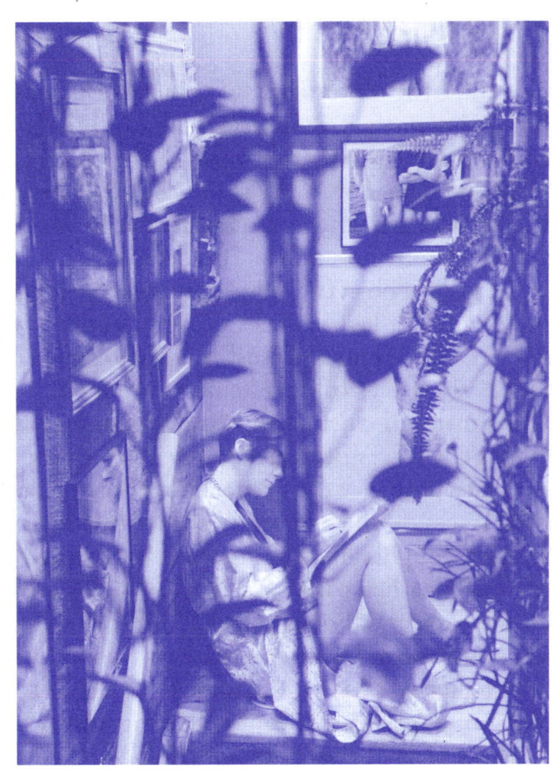

As part of a research action in the Montreal home of Tom Waugh, a participant reads a book in Waugh's library found by following a score scripted by Nemer. Photo: Benny Nemer.

JOHN POTVIN

Traces

Walter Benjamin, the chronicler of nineteenth-century Paris, deployed the notion of the trace as the residue of inhabitation, the physical remnants left behind, imprinted on the objects that populate the bourgeois home. For its occupant, the home became a credible and crucial space to compensate for life in the ever-expanding urban arena. Benjamin noted how "[i]ndefatigably, he takes the impression of a host of objects; for his slippers and his watches, his blankets and his umbrellas, he devises coverlets and cases. He has marked preference for velour and plush, which preserve the imprint of all contact... The traces of its inhabitant are moulded into the interior."[8] This material culture, to which we must certainly add books, provides the traces or evidence necessary in the detection and unfolding of a profile of the occupant. As documents of living, books provide traces of inhabitation in that some are dustier than others. A move through a library is marked by a series of physical contacts, of touch (leather, paper and cloth), which leave their own traces, as do the choices of books collected. All conjure the profile of the library's custodian.

Indeed, Nemer is himself a chronicler of these traces, here meant to conjure a queer archive of collecting and sexuality specific to the spaces of the private library. After all, the library operates as a permissive space, a space for lovers devoid of judgment or shame, a kind of "bibliosexuality," according to Nemer. Its books also serve as conduits to ancestral traces, links to a queer past. *I Don't Know Where Paradise Is* generously reaches back into the past, striving to forge a queer archive that retains indelible links.

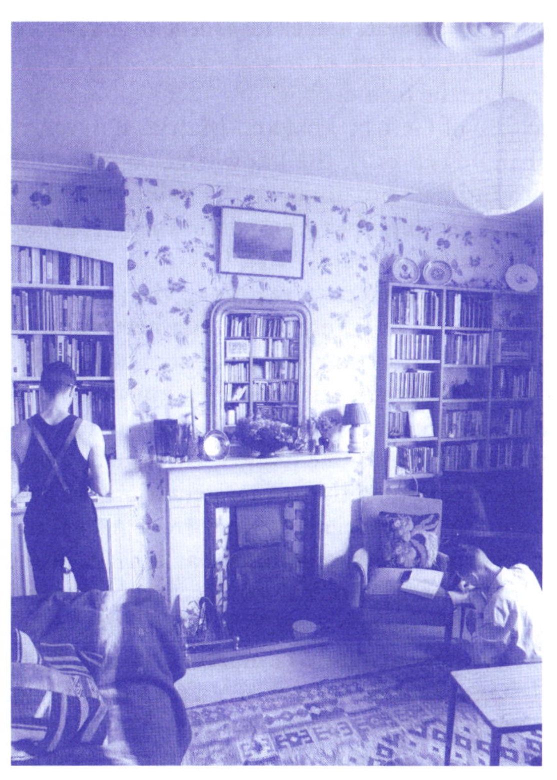

Participants navigate Adrian Rifkin's library by following a score scripted by Nemer. Photo: Benny Nemer.

By attempting to excavate queer ideas lost over time Nemer also questions the mechanisms of how to access this information in order to navigate the future.

In the case of Gert Hekma and Mattias Duyves, their home library—or more expressly, the knowledge contained therein—is brought into intimate proximity to the public sexual space of the urinal, blurring the lines between public and private, sensual and practical. In the chapter aptly titled "Urinal," Nemer discusses the public urinal located across the canal, visible from the couple's library. The connection is further maintained within the library itself, which hosts a section on queer sex and public urinals—Duyves is a scholar of the sexual history of the urinal. As Ian Scott Todd points out, the lavatory has functioned as a pivotal space in the history of queer lives and equally within queer literary history: "Having figured prominently in representations of gay male culture throughout the twentieth century from Jean Genet to Tom of Finland, the space of the lavatory has long been supposed to inspire a certain erotic, though not necessarily romantic, frisson within the gay male imagination."[9] Indeed, public toilets and urinals also became sites of a form of literary exchange in housing the names and messages exchanged between men seeking out the comfort of strangers. In Hekma and Duyves's Amsterdam library, both sexual and intellectual shame are staved off. All is permissible and celebrated as if to conjure the infamous eighteenth-century boudoir before bourgeois notions of respectability took hold—where sexuality, philosophy and space cavorted seamlessly.

In Nemer's queer spatiality, links between seemingly incompatible spaces—within a normative world order—have sexual,

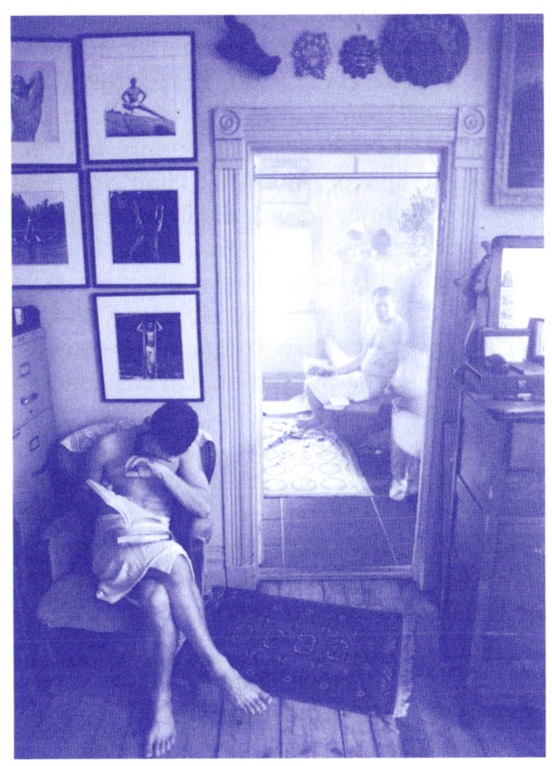

The sensory and affective dimensions of a bathhouse were recreated in Tom Waugh's home as part of Nemer's research action. Photo: Benny Nemer.

intellectual and even phenomenological spatial affinities, affective connections, necessary and liberatory interdependence. In an earlier project for Adrian Rifkin's London library, for example, Nemer created a "navigational score" rather than an audio guide. The score invited guests to select books of erotic promise and to transcribe a short passage into the score booklet.[10] Here Nemer called upon visitors to consciously and purposefully insert their sexuality into the process and experience of the space of the libraries. His participant-driven staging of Tom Waugh's library was conveniently located down the road from the Bain Coloniale, an all-male space where Jewish, Russian and Queer communities converge and that served as a direct source of inspiration. Given Nemer's interest in the queer history of the bathhouse, the proximity of Waugh's private library to the public bathhouse lent itself to a recreation of the spatial specificity of the two spaces coming together. A bathhouse-like environment was staged with the use of steam, visitors were free to shower and all were given towels. Visitors were also given a score and then went to the library in search of a passage of text to transcribe.[11]

From Library to Floral Arrangements

On the occasion of the exhibition at CUAG, Nemer, curator Heather Anderson and educator Fiona Wright invited members of Ottawa's 2SLGBTQ+ (Two-Spirit, lesbian, gay, bisexual, transgender, questioning, queer, intersex, pansexual, androgynous and asexual) community to create weekly floral arrangements that were exhibited in the gallery—even during pandemic closures—and that circulated as photographs on social media. The floral arrangements coincided with, and were made in response to, the release of a new chapter of the audio guide featured on CUAG's website. Like the audio guide with its cast of narrators, these floral arrangements underscored the way in which Nemer's work and the exhibition are devoted to the idea of anthology that is a set of voices, rather than an authoritative voice. To offset the negative effects of the physical and emotional toll of the pandemic, these beautiful and innovative floral concoctions stood in as a form of surrogate for individual and collective emotional responses as well as for the libraries and interiors themselves.

Floral arrangements have long provided an important conduit for queer sentiment and expression. In *I Don't Know Where Paradise Is*, the roots of the floral arrangements are many, I suggest. Initially they refer to the over twenty visits Nemer made to Hekma and Duyves's home. On each of these occasions, Nemer brought along flowers that were in turn preserved by the couple. Like the arrangements located at CUAG, these floral remnants formed the ephemeral traces of queer kinship endemic to the artist's project over time and across space (separated by an ocean). This notion of queer kinship necessarily leads us back to the important legacy left by celebrated queer floral designer and author Constance Spry (1886–1960), the doyenne of twentieth-century floral design. The weekly contributions re-appropriate the stereotype of the queer floral designer, and celebrate it. Flowers—like libraries and their contents—provide a sort of open secret of desire, intimacy and attachment. After all, libraries hold many secrets...

JOHN POTVIN

1 José Esteban Muñoz, *Cruising Utopia: The Then and There of Queer Futurity* (New York: New York University Press, 2009), 7.
2 Six libraries formed Nemer's original research proposal, pared down to four for the purposes of the exhibition and audio guide.
3 Nemer programmed the audio guide app to always play the first and last chapters but to shuffle the middle chapters, so that each listening experience is different.
4 Elizabeth Freeman, *Time Binds: Queer Temporalities, Queer Histories* (Durham, NC: Duke University Press, 2010), 3.
5 John Potvin, *Bachelors of a Different Sort: Queer Aesthetics, Material Culture and the Modern Interior in Britain* (Manchester, UK: Manchester University Press, 2014).
6 John Potvin, "Aesthetic Interiors within Institutional Interiors: The Art of Contemporary Queer Interventions," in Deborah Schneiderman, Anca I. Lasc and Karin Tehve (eds.), *Appropriated Interiors* (London, UK: Routledge, 2021).
7 Benny Nemer, *I Don't Know Where Paradise Is: Queer Paths through Museums and Libraries* (PhD diss., University of Edinburgh, 2020), 169.
8 Walter Benjamin, "Paris: Capital of the Nineteenth Century," in Rolf Tiedemann (ed.), *The Arcades Project* (Cambridge, MA: Belknap Press of Harvard University Press, 1999), 19–20.
9 Ian Scott Todd, "Christopher Isherwood's Bathroom," *Journal of Modern Literature* 38, no. 4, Spaces and Places (Summer 2015): 111.
10 This was an event in 2018 at which scores were presented as part of Benny's thesis exhibition at the University of Edinburgh's Playfair Library.
11 This was an event that formed part of Benny's thesis exhibition at the University of Edinburgh's Playfair Library.

SOMEONE IS WEEPING IN THE LIBRARY

BENNY NEMER

I am sitting on a pale-blue stepladder in a quiet corner of the library, the threshold between Gert and Mattias's book collection and their balcony garden, and I am crying.

I had been flipping through a copy of *The Young and the Evil*, a story from 1933 written by Charles Henri Ford and Parker Tyler, which Gert had pulled out for me from a bookshelf in the bedroom. I wouldn't have found it myself because the Ds, Es and Fs on the gay fiction shelves are arranged in a second row hidden behind the As, Bs and Cs. I had never heard of Ford but was enchanted by an interview with him in volume 1 of *Gay Sunshine Interviews*, which I had found the night before in a cabinet devoted to anthologies above the toilet. Ford chats casually about his enviable Paris set: the surrealist René Crevel, whom he met at one of Gertrude Stein's salons, and Edith Sitwell, who introduced him to the great love of his life, the painter Pavel Tchelitchew. He conjures an image of Djuna Barnes in a Tangier of yesteryear:

> She had finished *Nightwood,* and I was typing it for her. I found a home in the Casbah, and Djuna came down from Paris and lived with me there and our daily routine was that I would go to the beach in the morning, come back and have lunch, type in the afternoon. I don't know if I finished the book before she went back to Paris or not.[1]

The anthology was published by the author and pioneering gay publisher Winston Leyland, whose name surfaces repeatedly in my peregrinations through the library. His influence seems extensive and diverse: he appears as the publisher of a book about consent in sadomasochism called *The Kiss of the Whip*; he is credited as the editor of a book of gay Latin American fiction entitled *My Deep Dark Pain Is Love*; he is thanked in the translator's notes for a collection of homoerotic poetry by the eighth-century Persian poet Abū Nūwas. When I open another book, a typed letter addressed to Gert falls out, written by Leyland himself in 1994: he is searching for an apartment in Amsterdam; he is working on a Dutch translation of Paul Verlaine; he signs off "yours in affectionate comradeship in gay liberation, Winston."

My hand drifts from the anthology to a book of photographs by Rotimi Fani-Kayode that opens to an image of a young Black man against a saffron-coloured background. His face and torso are enveloped and partly concealed by delicate branches dense with baby's breath, which veil the expression in his eyes. The image is printed as a small square at the bottom corner of an otherwise blank page, like photographic marginalia, as though marginalized by design. The title of the artwork takes up more page space than the image itself: *Nothing to Lose X (Bodies of Experience)*. The photograph is from 1989, the year of Fani-Kayode's death from AIDS.

I open a book entitled *Oceanic Homosexualities* to a chapter about a shaman from an Indigenous Siberian community—a "woman transformed into a man"—who fastens the calf muscle of a deer to himself with a leather belt, using it as a strap-on dildo with which to penetrate his wife.[2] The shaman is one of a number of precolonial Indigenous sexual and gender identities the book documents: identities and practices that did not conform to a binary, heterosexual organization of relations while not necessarily being classified as non-normative by the societies in which they

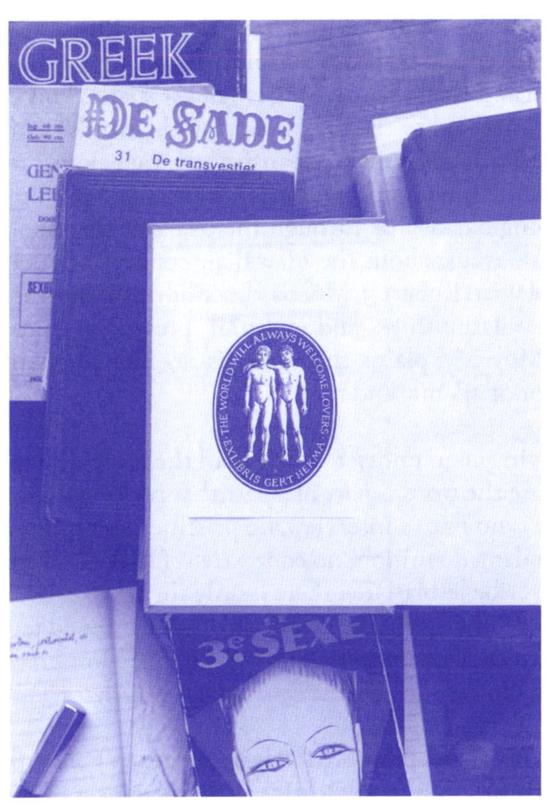

Gert Hekma's Ex Libris *label on the*
inside cover of a book found during Nemer's research.
Photo: Benny Nemer.

lived. I do not remember why I had selected this particular book, or what had led me here. I was simply browsing the library, cruising around and then approaching whatever sparked my curiosity. I was likely attracted to the title, believing the word "oceanic" to be meant poetically to signify "expansive" or "capacious," rather than to indicate the geographic region of Oceania.

Flipping backwards through the pages of this book, my eyes settle on a passage about the Hawaiian concept of aikāne, which the ethnologist Robert J. Morris describes as denoting same-sex identities, relationships and cultural presences in precolonial Hawai'i. Morris explains that there is no English equivalent for the concept of aikāne, and that,

> [a]rriving at an understanding is all the more difficult because the word is part of a past that no longer exists. There is no one to interview, no pristine chief or his aikāne to render a definition; no context; no Hiiaka and company to describe lesbian life; there is only the text—a text, incidentally, originally meant only to be listened to. So one understands the prayer: "O ko mākou mau kūpuna keia lā, pehea iho la ia lā." O Ancestors, what was that time like?[3]

It is the words of this prayer that trigger my tears. For despite having no direct connection to the worlds and experiences of the Siberian shaman or the other figures documented in this book, I feel an ancestral link to them, a stream of longing that connects my twenty-first-century gay body to theirs, to Winston's, Rotimi's, Charles's, Djuna's. My tears are for the extinction and erasure of these and

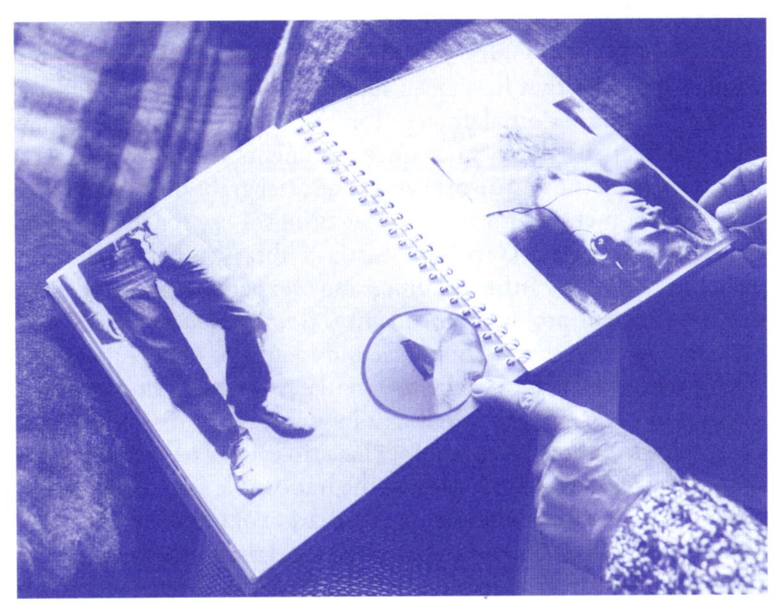

*Adrian Rifkin handles
a collage album in the library of his London home.
Photo: Benny Nemer.*

so many other identities and practices that might be classified as *queer* in contemporary parlance; for all the beautiful expressions of sexuality that have been suppressed over time by religious, patriarchal and colonial forces; for the impossibility of retrieving the affects of these other queer moments in time and space.

As is often the nature of crying, one grief grabs hold of another, and I am soon crying for many other things. I cry for the magnificent labyrinth that is Gert and Mattias's library, for the sensation of being lost in its infinite dimensions, experiencing Jorge Luis Borges's "ancient problem: *The Library is unlimited and cyclical.*"[4] I cry for my wish for the histories and identities of the queer kin who dwell within the library to circulate, for modern-day queer identity to be firmly grounded in a long lineage of dissonant practices, subverted norms and an inexhaustible array of sexual expressions. I cry tears of exasperation at the impossible scale of the task I have set for myself: an audio guide mediation of Gert and Mattias's library, a tour that somehow documents and shares the treasures of queerness that their collection houses; an artwork that acts as an agent of the kind of queer consciousness I wish to foster.

It is my seventh visit to the library in two years, yet I have never felt further from my goal. I expected myself capable of creating a tour that told some kind of documentary truth, that spoke from a position of knowing, embodying the "expert position" that audio guides traditionally assume, transmitting knowledge as a didactic gesture. But the fact is that I do not know, and the more time I spend in the library, the less I seem to know, or the less stable my knowledge becomes. For every time I take a turn in the library, each time I open a book, someone is waiting for me. The library is full of ancestors too vast to compile, too oceanic to grasp. I feel like an imposter: a searcher posing as a guide.

Describing the use of memoirs and biographies as source material in his study of the interior spaces of British gay men from 1885 to 1957, John Potvin articulates the limits of historical documents produced from an outsider position: "Biographies are only partial glimpses... perceptions based solely on a position as outsider, a sort of interloper within the spatial culture of the home."[5] Biographies make up only a portion of the materials Potvin worked from—which also included photographs and diaries—however, he acknowledges that reliable representation of some of the interiors in question were not always available, requiring him to modify his methods depending on the nature of his materials.

My artistic research into the libraries and interior spaces of a more contemporary (and mostly still living) group of gay men did not take the expressive form of biography, but Potvin's warning that the outsider's perspective can only ever offer a partial glance is of relevance to both my methods and my vision of the artistic outcome of my research. I was for the most part invited into these homes to conduct my weird research by the homeowners themselves, so I was not an interloper, but rather a kind of benevolent acquaintance: a reader, a student, a guest, with all the attendant affects and relations that accompany these identities. Yet something about an interloper positionality resonates, and I sense some generative potential in acknowledging and exploring the illegitimated positions of both outsider and interloper, subjectivities that seem decidedly queer, echoing David Halperin's assertion of queerness being "at odds with the normal, the legitimate, the dominant."[6]

To assume an interloper positionality might be to recognize the limits of what about these spaces I can ever expect to understand or portray and might also serve as an embodied methodological position that informs the content and aesthetics of my artistic work. There is a link here to my interest in the care and stewardship of queer historical materials, for as much as my research is driven by a desire to share what I have found in the libraries of my hosts, I also feel a protective impulse, a concern that not everything should be revealed or made public, that the didactic amplification that is the raison d'être of a museum audio guide is perhaps not appropriate here. Some of my encounters in the library belong in an artwork, others belong in my diary, and others are opaque to me, and are only for my hosts to know, experience and feel. Furthermore, there are some libraries to which I never gained access, despite significant correspondence and arrangements with their keepers. Besides, I often felt I did not belong in the scholarly setting of these libraries, not only because of my ignorance of the histories and ideas they contain, but because of the feelings of confusion and despair I often felt over how to navigate within them. I felt I was merely *performing* the role of reader, performing the role of scholar, even performing my role as artist.

I attempted to mitigate these imposterish feelings by offering my hosts bouquets, distracting attention from my inability to articulate the goals of my research by focusing on the sensory pleasures of flowers. Floral gifts acted as a kind of social lubricant, bringing me closer to my hosts by discussing the arrangement or selecting vases from their collections. A bouquet of dahlias prompted Adrian Rifkin to invite me to see his garden during my first research

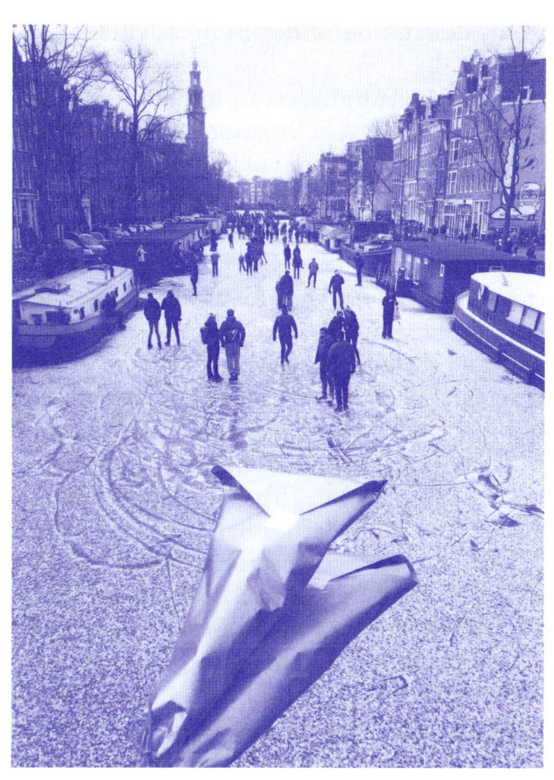

Transporting bouquets of flowers on the way to a research visit at the Amsterdam home of Gert Hekma and Mattias Duyves. Photo: Benny Nemer.

visit, where his description of designing a "child-unfriendly" garden became the basis of our first conversation of substance. Green chrysanthemums provided an initial topic of conversation when arriving at the home of Christine Seemüller—the devisee of Hervé Guibert's estate and keeper of his library—offering a subject of discussion in which I felt more fluent than with Guibert's biography and literary oeuvre. René Schérer was initially overwhelmed by my gift of purple and white spotted orchids, explaining that he had nowhere to put them. But once a vase was found, the act of arranging the flowers together become one of our few moments of connection and shared embodiment—at least in my experience.

As my research into the relational aspects of the audio guide and museum mediation deepened, I came to understand these floral gifts, and the social and relational exchange they fostered, as central to my artistic research. This observation crystallized in the realization that Gert and Mattias had kept many of the arrangements I had offered them over the years, displaying them as a kind of permanent exhibition (or perhaps mausoleum) of the gifts that had punctuated my research visits. Seeing my encounters with them and their home immortalized and integrated into the culture and holdings of their collection had a profound effect on me and deepened my awareness of the importance of the relationships I had cultivated with my hosts, not just to my personal life, but to the research at hand. Themes of kinship have always fuelled this project, although I mostly sought out kinship bonds with the authors and figures who appeared in the books I found, like the Siberian shaman in *Oceanic Homosexualities*. I was more invested in what Heather Love refers to as "backward glances" into the

Touch this book and let it touch you. Press a finger against its spine. If you feel the book is willing – if the book appears to be as interested in you as you are in it – pull it down from the shelf and into your hands. Finger its pages. Get into its contours and textures. Stroke its skin. Stay aware of how the book touches you as you touch it.

Kiss the book. Yes, bring it to your mouth. Press the

ex libris label to your lips.
Don't be shy. It's natural
that you should feel aroused
in the library, among all its
sexy words and images.
Besides, there is surely no
environment more permissive
than this one. You are in
the company of all the perverts
in history. You are in a
world that welcomes lovers.
No one here would ever think
to judge your act of
bibliosexuality.

queer past, instrumentalizing my present-tense relationships with my hosts in order to do my research.[7]

In this way, feeling like an imposter had a generative effect on my research, a source of action that Maddie Breeze asserts as part of a feminist reimagining of existing modes of knowledge production:

> I want to move away from understanding "imposter syndrome" as a personal problem of faulty self-esteem inviting individualized coping solutions and see what happens when we situate feelings of imposterism in socio-political context ... and think of feeling like an imposter as a potential source of action and site of agency.[8]

Feelings of imposterism are likely less acute in the sociopolitical context of self-directed artistic research than for feminist scholars navigating the patriarchal hierarchies of neo-liberal universities—the context in which Breeze makes this assertion—making the problem I faced in the libraries perhaps less structural. But it was the "individualized coping solutions" I developed to mask my own imposter syndrome—namely the introduction of floral gifts—that became such a rich and integral part of my research.

Over time, I was increasingly folded into the lives of my hosts, socializing with them while conducting research and participating in domestic tasks like yard work and hanging framed artworks on their walls. During my research visits to his home, Adrian Rifkin would jokingly tell visitors that I was his gardener. I joined Tom Waugh and his friends at their weekly bathhouse outings and slept in his guest room when conducting research in Montreal. I also periodically slept at Adrian and Denis's home during research visits to London, notably on a daybed in the library. I took cuttings from my hosts' plant collections and am now nurturing a *Ficus drupacea pubescens* from Amsterdam, a spider plant from Montreal and an anthurium from London in my own home.

This increasing intimacy with my hosts at once confused and enriched my working methods, and my sense of being an interloper or imposter subsided and transformed as I began to feel like a friend doing research rather than a researcher being friendly. Momentary feelings of exasperation in the libraries still sometimes surfaced, but by allowing my relationships and affective impulses to more actively lead my research, my attitude towards methods of knowledge production shifted the goals of the project, as well as what aspect of the libraries, homes and encounters with my hosts felt most important to portray. I believe I have developed what Trinh T. Minh-ha refers to as a "critical not-knowingness" that feels generative not only for my specific research into these homes and collections, but also for the greater project of reimagining the museum audio guide, of diminishing and dispersing its authoritative voice.[9] And if my sleepovers, bathhouse outings and floral gifts can be recognized as legitimate modes of embodied research, then surely I can also make methodological room for my tears.

BENNY
NEMER

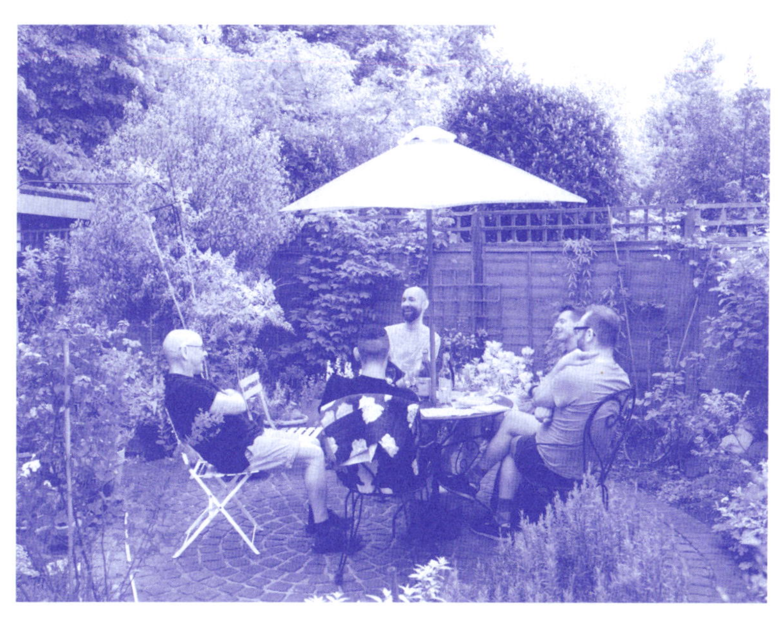

Nemer in conversation with Adrian Rifkin and participants of his research action in Rifkin's garden. Photo: Ed Twaddle.

1 Charles Henri Ford, "Charles Henri Ford" interview by Iran Cohen, in *Gay Sunshine Interviews*, vol. 1, edited by Winston Leyland (San Francisco: Gay Sunshine Press, 1978), 40.

2 Stephen O. Murray, "Vladimir Bogoraz's Account of Chukchi Transformed Shamans," in *Oceanic Homosexualities*, edited by Stephen O. Murray (New York: Garland Publishing, 1992), 306.

3 Robert J. Morris, "Same-Sex Friendships in Hawaiian Lore: Constructing the Canon," in *Oceanic Homosexualities*, 75.

4 Jorge Luis Borges, *Labyrinths* (Cambridge, MA: New Directions, 1962), 58. Emphasis in original.

5 John Potvin, *Bachelors of a Different Sort: Queer Aesthetics, Material Culture and the Modern Interior in Britain* (Manchester: Manchester University Press, 2014), 7.

6 David Halperin, *Saint Foucault: Towards a Gay Hagiography* (Oxford and New York: Oxford University Press, 1995), 62.

7 Heather Love, *Feeling Backward: Loss and the Politics of Queer History* (Cambridge, MA: Harvard University Press, 2007).

8 Maddie Breeze, "Imposter Syndrome as a Public Feeling," in *Feeling Academic in the Neoliberal University*, edited by Yvette Taylor and Kinneret Lahad, Palgrave Studies in Gender and Education (New York: Springer International Publishing, 2018), 201.

9 Trinh T. Minh-Ha, *When the Moon Waxes Red: Representation, Gender and Cultural Politics* (London and New York: Routledge, 1991).

DIRECTOR'S AFTERWORD

SANDRA DYCK

I was working from home on a brisk winter's day in early 2021. The Covid-19 Omicron variant was rampant, vaccines had not yet been released, Ottawa was in lockdown and CUAG was closed. The doorbell rang and I opened the door to a delivery person standing on the porch, holding a flower arrangement heavily wrapped against the elements. The bouquet, it turns out, had been sent by another gallery that I'd been collaborating with closely, thanking me for my work. I set the flowers on my desk and basked in their delicate beauty for days. I sometimes scroll through the photographic archive on my mobile phone to find images of that bouquet, not only to summon its beauty but also to reconnect to the joy and surprise I felt as the fortunate recipient of an extraordinary gift.

In "Someone Is Weeping in the Library," his essay for this book, Benny Nemer reflects on the power of floral gifts in *I Don't Know Where Paradise Is*. The flowers he brought to his first meetings with scholars and collectors he'd never met but longed to work with helped him navigate the nervous early moments of such social encounters. Over time, the bouquets came to symbolize not only the building of these relationships and the rewards of doing so, but also the processes of exchange so fundamental to his project—the sharing of different knowledges, experiences and ideas, and worlds.

We often speak of floral bouquets as arrangements. Reimagining and producing *I Don't Know Where Paradise Is* in Ottawa during the first year of a global pandemic, which involved many collaborators separated from Nemer by the Atlantic Ocean, required a lot of arrangements. When I think back to the twenty-six floral compositions created during the project, though, I think of how their gorgeous, affecting and often startling constituent parts collectively arranged and embodied the labour and love of everyone involved.

I am grateful to Benny Nemer and exhibition curator Heather Anderson for their flexibility, creativity and resilience in realizing this extraordinary project. Public health restrictions prevented us from bringing Benny to Ottawa or hosting an in-person vernissage, so we celebrated with a party livestreamed from the gallery, produced by Fiona Wright, hosted by Glenn Nuotio and featuring a botanical cocktail mixed at the event. Benny and Ann Cvetkovich engaged in a lively conversation. Well-wishers joined online from several countries in a gathering that poignantly bridged physical distances.

I Don't Know Where Paradise Is unfolded in the gallery and online over thirteen weeks, each culminating in the gift of an audio work and two floral arrangements. CUAG invited six local partners—Vincent Edet, Bill Brown and John McKinven (together), Lydia Collins, Benny Michaud and Sam Loewen—to work with the florist and educator Kat Kosk to realize their unique visions. Their synergistic labour of arranging flowers anchored the exhibition at CUAG socially, materially and in real time. Jason Laguerre, an emerging photographer and member of the gallery's front desk team, worked with the lens-based artist Olivia Johnson to document the arrangements; Jason's role was generously supported by the Mame Jackson Experiential Learning Fund. Fiona Wright expertly managed exhibition communications and behind-the-scenes logistics.

This book, designed by Paris-based Clément Wibaut, beautifully arranges the sonic, textual, photographic and floral elements of *I Don't Know Where Paradise Is.* Essays by Heather Anderson, Ann Cvetkovich, Jennifer Evans, Benny Nemer and John Potvin astutely situate the work of this project within broader, overlapping contexts. The Ottawa-based collaborators contributed brief texts reflecting on their individual experiences (which we originally shared with subscribers to CUAG's electronic mailing list during the exhibition's run). Lydia Collins, a poet and sexual health educator wrote that she, too, didn't know the location of paradise. Benny Nemer's project, she concluded, came close to finding it. That is a gift.

CONTRIBUTORS

BENNY NEMER

Benny Nemer is an artist and diarist based in Paris. Born in Montreal in 1973, he is the grandson of Quebec potter Rosalie Namer (1925–2006), whose artistic kinship instilled in him an early aesthetic sensibility that included an appreciation of objects, a practice of epistolary writing and a sympathy with flowers.

Early experiences of homophobia and gender disciplining had an enduring impact on Nemer's identity, artistic impulses and political orientations, as did an adolescent fear of and fascination with the AIDS crisis. Nemer sang in youth choirs and briefly studied ballet, experiences that provided the material for his first body of performance-based work. His emergence as a professional artist was facilitated by the queer art scene of 1990s Toronto and the support of artists including Kim Fullerton, Lisa Steele and Vera Frenkel, as well as institutions like Vtape, Inside Out and the Images Festival, where he was awarded the title *Art Fag 2000* at the turn of the millennium.

In search of new sensations, Nemer moved to Berlin in 2001, changing the artistic, sexual and relational landscape of his life and work. His artistic development advanced through participation in numerous residencies, notably in Innsbruck, Stockholm, New York, Vienna and Paris, as well as an MFA at Concordia University mentored by Ingrid Bachman, Nancy Ring and Tom Waugh. Nemer credits the evolution of his artistic voice to friendships he has maintained with artists including Aleesa Cohene, August Klintberg, Conny Karlsson Lundgren, Pascal Lièvre, Stephen Thompson, Alisha Piercy and Jonathan VanDyke, as well as close relationships with curators, among them Heather Anderson, Albin Hillervik, Jane Becker Nelson, Seán Elder Wilson, Ashkan Sephavand, Blair Todd, Patrik Steorn and Tarin Dehod, who created unique conditions for him to dream and take artistic risks.

Nemer's fascination with performance-based video expanded to multidisciplinary practice concerned with queer archives and relational gestures, taking form through sound, participatory actions, epistolary writing and floral arranging. His artworks often trace the affective contours of love and longing while facilitating bonds of kinship between his audience, figures from history and himself.

A turn in Nemer's practice toward the museum audio guide as an artistic format resulted in collaborations with the Kunsthistorisches Museum (Vienna), POLIN Museum of the History of Polish Jews (Warsaw) and Thielska Galleriet (Stockholm). He completed a practice-led PhD at the Edinburgh College of Art in 2019, where he was part of *Cruising the Seventies: Unearthing Pre-HIV/AIDS Queer Sexual Cultures*, a pan-European research project led by art historians, cultural anthropologists and artists. Advised by film scholar Glyn Davis and art historian Fiona Anderson, Nemer's doctoral research critically examined the audio guide as a media form, turning to queer theory as well as museum mediation practice to expand and reimagine its potential. He is currently a postdoctoral researcher at KASK & Conservatorium in Ghent, Belgium, where he is pursuing research into queer kinship in the spectre of AIDS, postcards as an artistic medium and the archive of French author and photographer Hervé Guibert.

In addition to numerous private collections, Nemer's work is in the permanent collections of the National Gallery of Canada, the Ystads Konstmuseum and the Flaten Art Museum.

ESSAYISTS

Heather Anderson

is Curator at Carleton University Art Gallery. She first presented the work of Benny Nemer when Assistant Curator in the Contemporary Art Department at the National Gallery of Canada. Her recent exhibitions include *Laura Taler: THREE SONGS* (2022) and *The Baroness Elsa Project* (2021). Her recent exhibition publications include *Carol Sawyer: The Natalie Brettschneider Archive* (2020) and *Rebecca Belmore: March 5, 1819* (2018).

Ann Cvetkovich

is a professor in the Feminist Institute of Social Transformation at Carleton University. Her books include *An Archive of Feelings: Trauma, Sexuality, and Lesbian Public Cultures* (2003) and *Depression: A Public Feeling* (2012); her co-edited anthologies include (with Janet Staiger and Ann Reynolds) *Political Emotions* (2010). She has served as co-editor, with Annamarie Jagose, of *GLQ: A Journal of Lesbian and Gay Studies*. Her recent writing projects focus on the current state of LGBTQ archives and their creative use by artists to create counter-archives and interventions in public history.

Jennifer Evans

is a professor of history at Carleton University. Her research and teaching focus on the history of sexuality, right-wing populism and authoritarianism, especially in the context of its evolution on social media and visual culture. In 2016 she was elected to the College of New Scholars, Royal Society of Canada. She has authored and edited several books including *The Queer Art of History: Queer Kinship After Fascism* (2023). She is currently working on *Photography and the Sexual Revolution: A Transnational Affair*.

John Potvin

is a professor of art history at Concordia University, where he teaches on the intersections of art, design and fashion. His research focuses on the ways the male body, competing masculinities and dissident sexualities are performed, represented, memorialized and perceived in modern design and material and visual cultures since the late nineteenth century in Europe and North America. His publications include *Bachelors of a Different Sort: Queer Aesthetics, Material Culture and the Modern Interior in Britain* (2014), which won the Historians of British Art Book Prize, and *Deco Dandy: Designing Masculinity in 1920s Paris* (2020).

FLORAL RESPONDENTS

CUAG invited the six members of the Ottawa-Gatineau Two-Spirit, Lesbian, Gay, Bisexual, Transgender, Queer+ community who created the floral arrangements featured in *I Don't Know Where Paradise Is* to contribute reflective texts on their participation in the project. These texts were shared through CUAG's e-newsletter, along with paired images of the previous week's floral arrangements—both theirs and Nemer's. The floral recipients' texts are presented here to offer insights into their experiences and gesture to how Nemer's collaborative approach to *I Don't Know Where Paradise Is* extends community and queer kinship.

Vincent Edet

These are the emotions that I experienced during the process of working on this project. To me, it was about seeing the world in a new perspective and being able to experience those feelings with a new art medium.

Can you feel it?
The wind, as it flows freely without a care.
As if tiptoes on every strain of grass
And taps every leaf equally.
She does not discriminate,
and she does not judge.
She is light and she is heavy.
I wonder, does the wind ever end?
Or does she just keep flowing?
We will never know, but I know that
One day I will be as free as the wind.
Touching all but never being
held down.

Vincent Edet is a Nigerian Canadian artist, model and designer. He graduated in 2020 from Carleton University with a degree in Criminology and Criminal Justice and a concentration in Psychology. You can find his work at @xvnctx.

Bill Brown and John McKinven

In Benny Nemer's world, silence contains sound, and words in their abundance fog over intimacy, which can sow confusion instead of clarity. Over time, we began to feel our way together, into some sort of fluency where our thoughts and images, in conversation with Kat Kosk, might, so to speak, encourage Benny's ideas to bloom. Our reflections, both alone and together, opened us up to new ideas about our middle-class life, hybridized years ago by our contradictions, our questions and our prickly understandings, and have fed daily conversations, over 6 p.m. cocktails, that whorl around our lives together. When strangers walk through our Ottawa gardens, they often call the front one an "oasis," the side one "magical"; we have imagined these folks a part of our project, the work of each other as a couple. Now we can imagine viewers of our two CUAG bouquets—at least those who question where to find words or who pay attention to the sounds of silence—as joining those ranks.

Bill Brown and John McKinven are art collectors and urban gardeners. For over thirty years they have lovingly created and tended the garden in front of the Windsor Arms, a heritage apartment building in a downtown residential Ottawa neighbourhood.

Lydia Collins

Participating in *I Don't Know Where Paradise Is* was such a lovely experience. Each audio chapter felt personal, discussing gardens of libraries, tall and lively plants, and brought a sense of comfort and belonging to queer life. This project was exciting, emotional and relatable. I often allowed my mind to wander into the spaces that the narrator's words brought me to: I laughed and cried and replayed. Benny has a certain warmth, not only in his work but in his whole being, which I could feel even with our only available means of communication being through emails, Zoom chats and Instagram messages. I too don't know where paradise is: it might be sunken into the soft couch corner with my partner, or in a freshly baked gluten-free lemon poppyseed loaf. I don't know where paradise is, but I think Benny's work came pretty damn close to finding it.

Lydia Collins is a poet, sexual health educator and community organizer. Her recent work, Joy Is Our Birthright, *is a collaborative project with UNILEARNAL that aims to capture Black joy, particularly among Black queer and trans people. Lydia is the author of three self-published chapbooks of poetry:* Angry. Black. Woman. *(2019),* To Everyone We've Ever Been *(2020) and* In Transit *(2021).*

Benny Michaud

I am struck by the contrast between sacred beings interpreted as aesthetic "objects" and the sanitized, disconnected spaces in which they are housed. Indigenous voices, stolen and kept for a privileged few, are presented behind glass and on stark pages—with the distant song of ancestors confused for the hum of concrete buildings.

"Cigarettes and Sweetgrass"

(for Paul)

detailed beading on his jacket
braided hair washed in kindness
denim on denim and,
his scent—
cigarettes and sweetgrass
dancing in the wind
tempting,
calling,
singing,
a teaching song "but how? I'm tired..."
Patience
leather boots crunching unforgiving white
eyes focused on a distant sky
his smoke drifting over the lake
and in the quiet before we move on
understanding settles
and a new story begins to form

Benny Michaud is a Two-Spirit Eagle clan Michif person. She is a citizen of the Metis Nation and director of the Centre for Indigenous Support and Community Engagement at Carleton University. Originally from Winnipeg, she now resides in unceded Algonquin territory.

Sam Loewen

I looked forward tremendously to the weekly gift of the audio chapters from Benny. When each chapter arrived, I listened to it repeatedly, meditating on his words. On each loop of the chapter, I wrote down observations and produced drawings of my emotional, bodily and intellectual responses and associations. These responses to the objects and spatial descriptions of the library usually focused on the ability of scents and textures to evoke memories. Throughout the listening process, it was important not to fixate on visual representations or rigid compositions. The aesthetic decisions were made collaboratively with florist Kat Kosk when we produced the final arrangements in the gallery. Instead, I offered Kat sensorial directives about the scent, feeling, aura or colours that each floral composition should include. I then contributed a personal item to adorn the arrangement: an amethyst stone, a rope of bedsheets, two tarot cards. These items symbolized the memories that were elicited during my meditation on each audio chapter.

Sam Loewen is a queer interdisciplinary artist and designer residing in Ottawa. His artistic practice explores methods of codification within Western culture to discuss queer "masculine" identities.

Kat Kosk began her floral arranging career in Dresden, Germany, in 1996. Her unique aesthetic and work as a florist, educator and owner of Ottawa's Blumenstudio have been acknowledged worldwide.

Benny Nemer

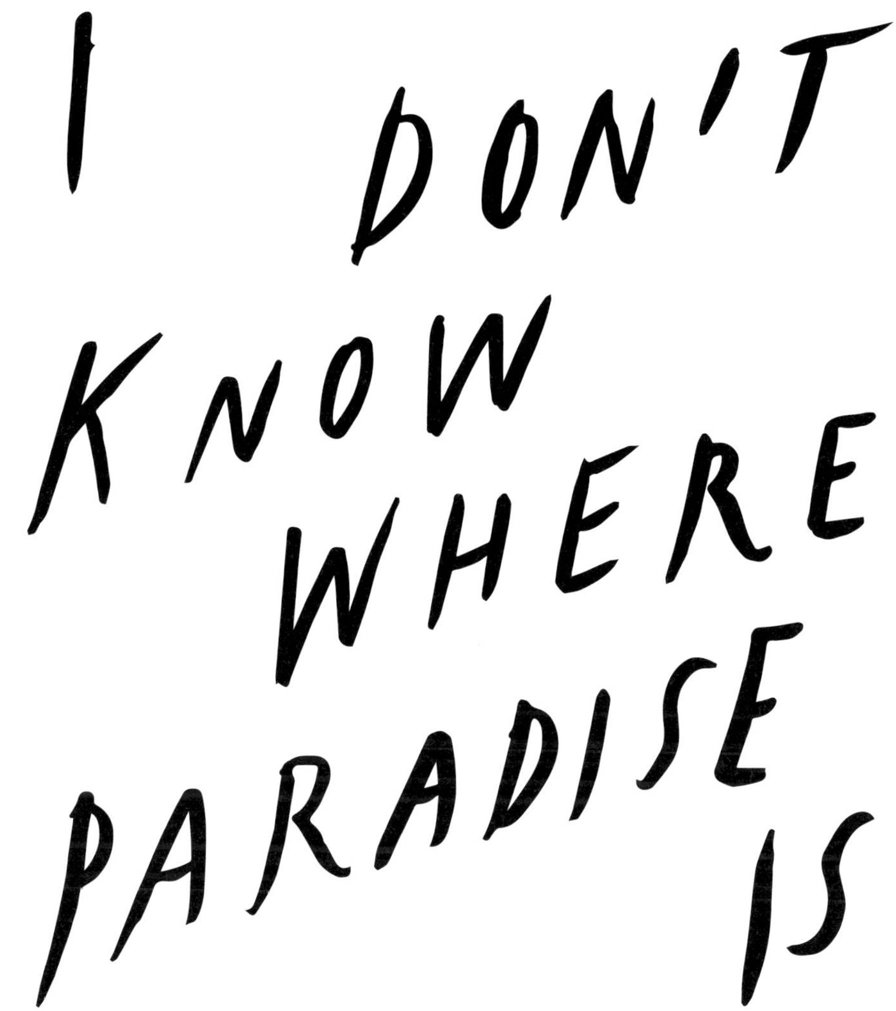

I Don't Know Where Paradise Is

Texts by Heather Anderson
Ann Cvetkovich Jennifer Evans
John Potvin

Carleton University Art Gallery

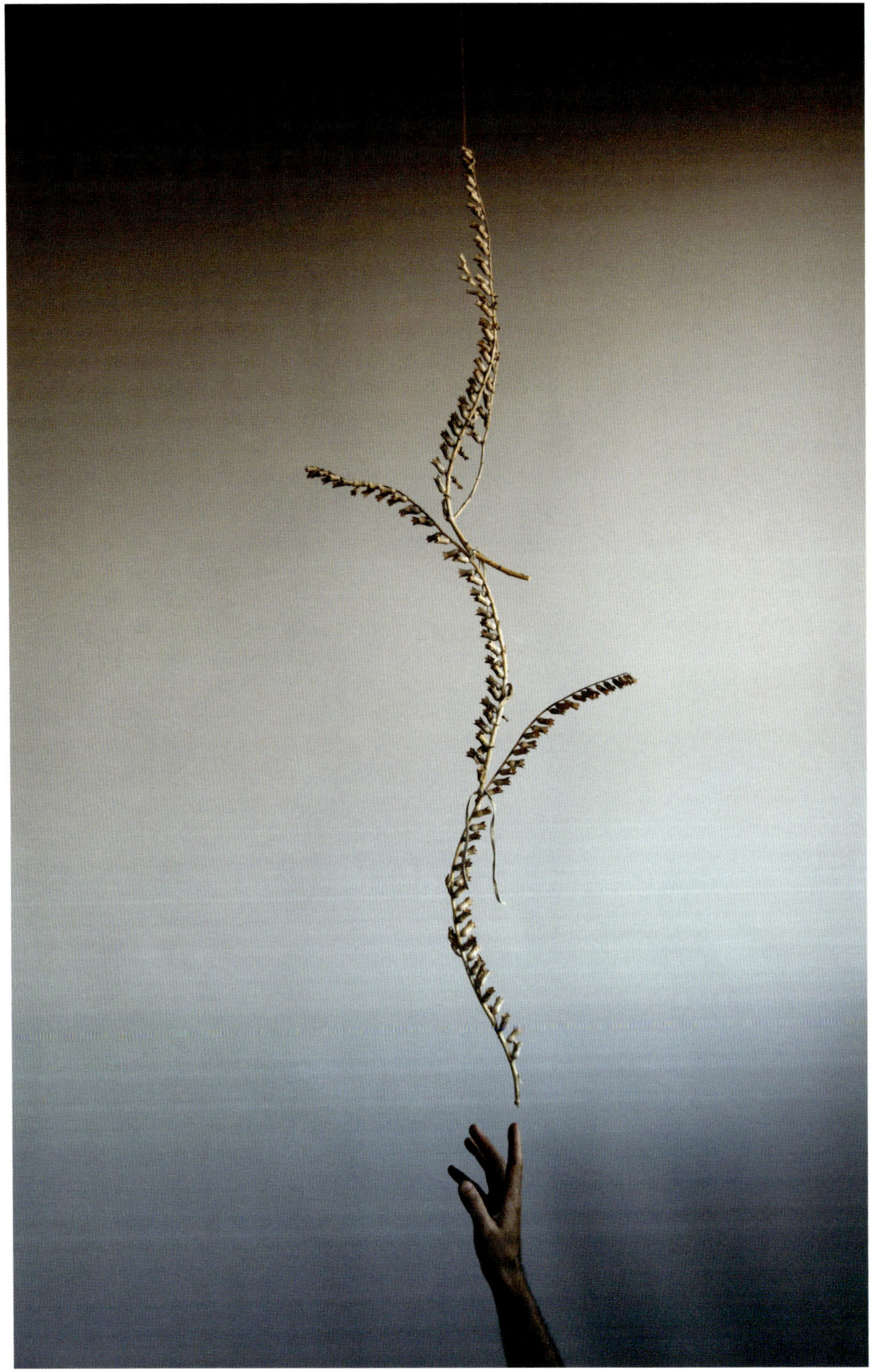

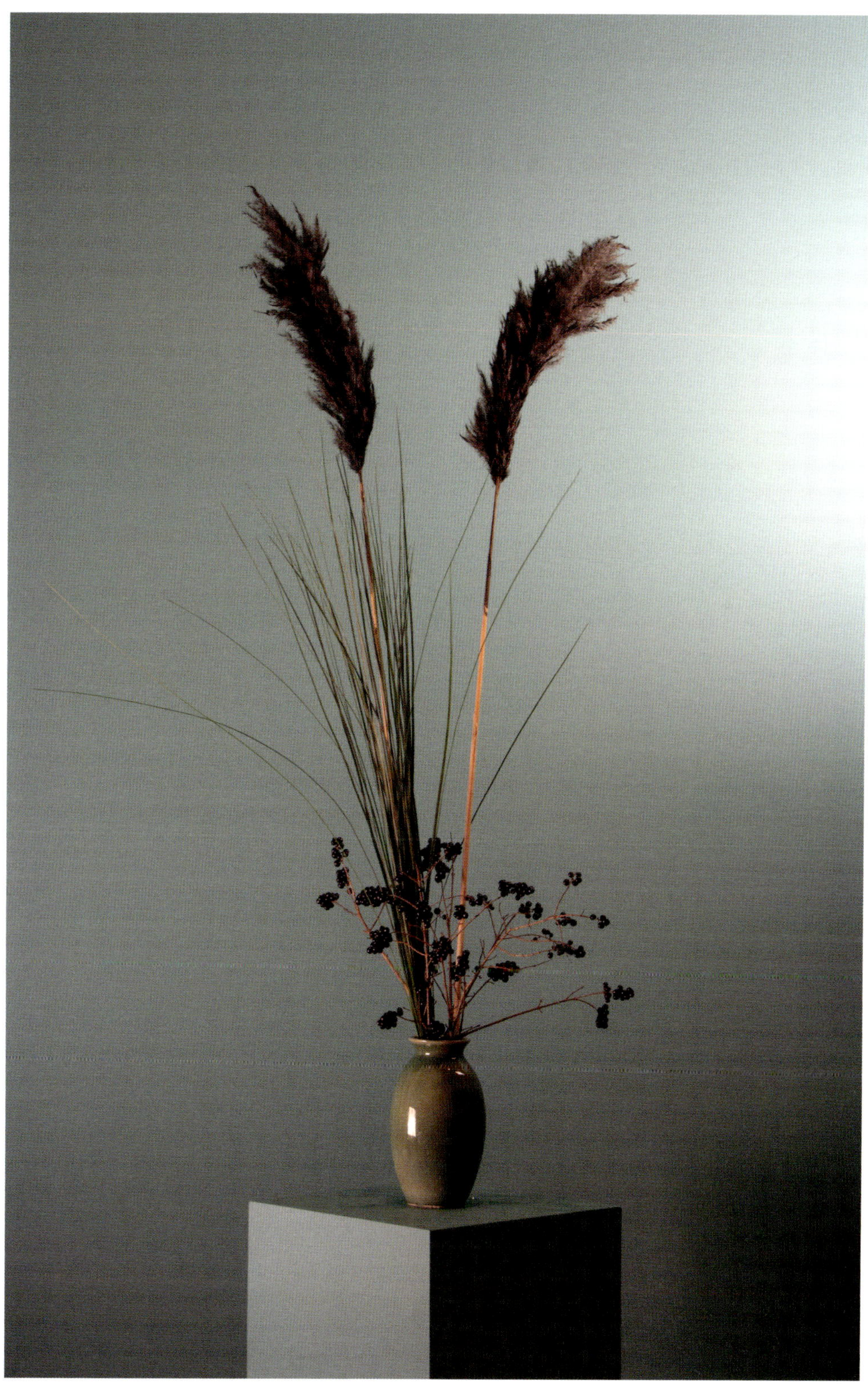

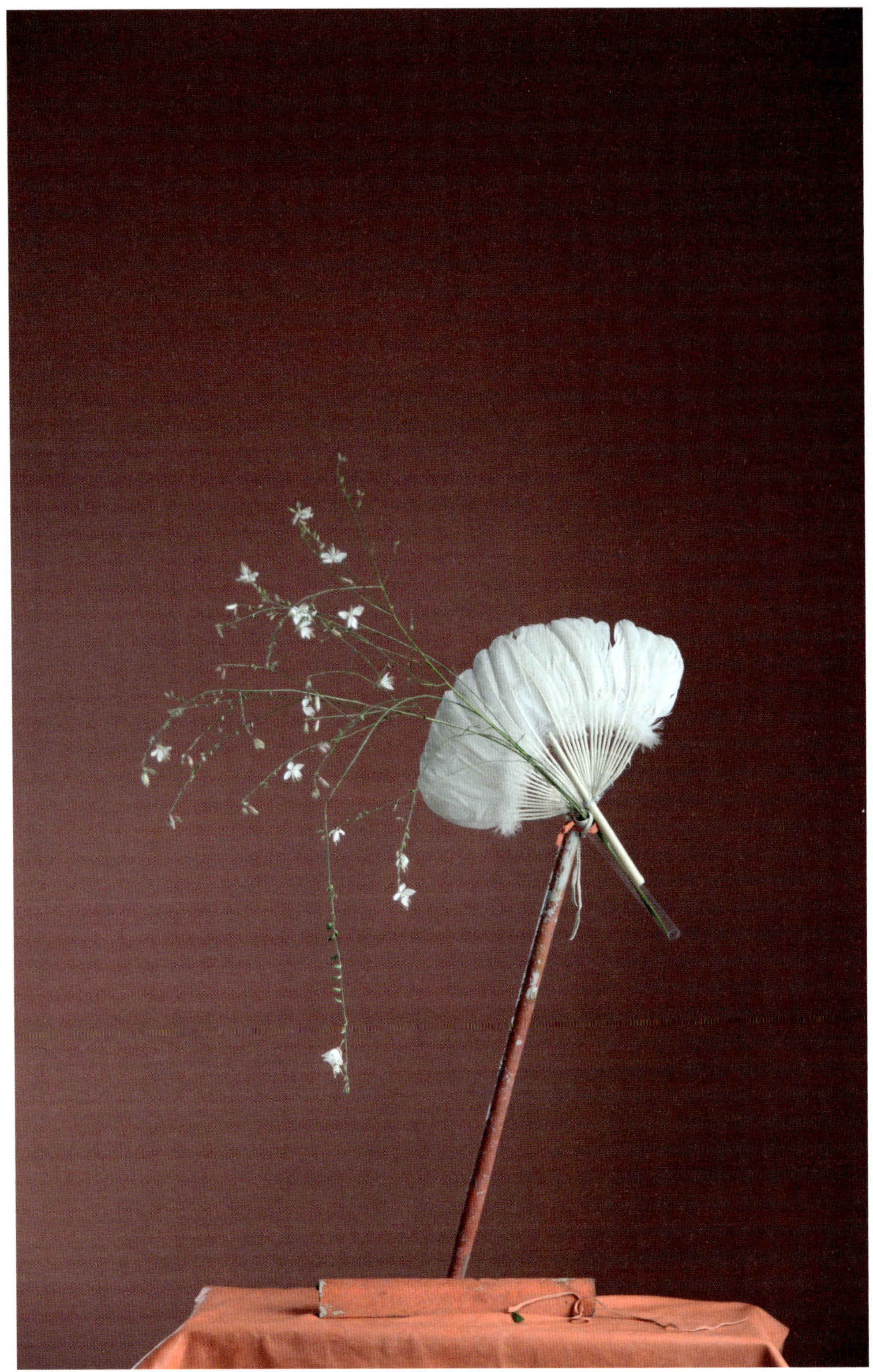

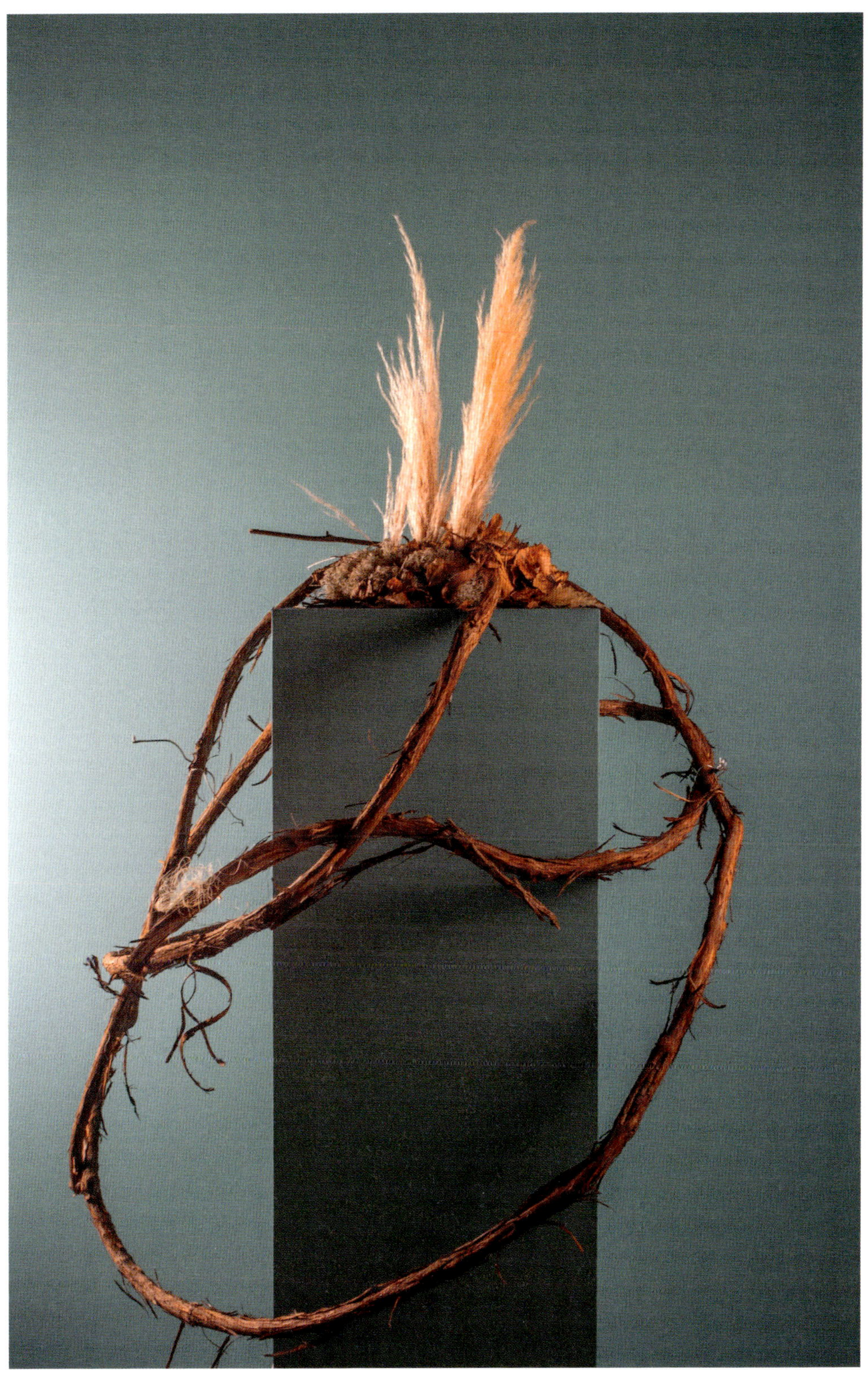

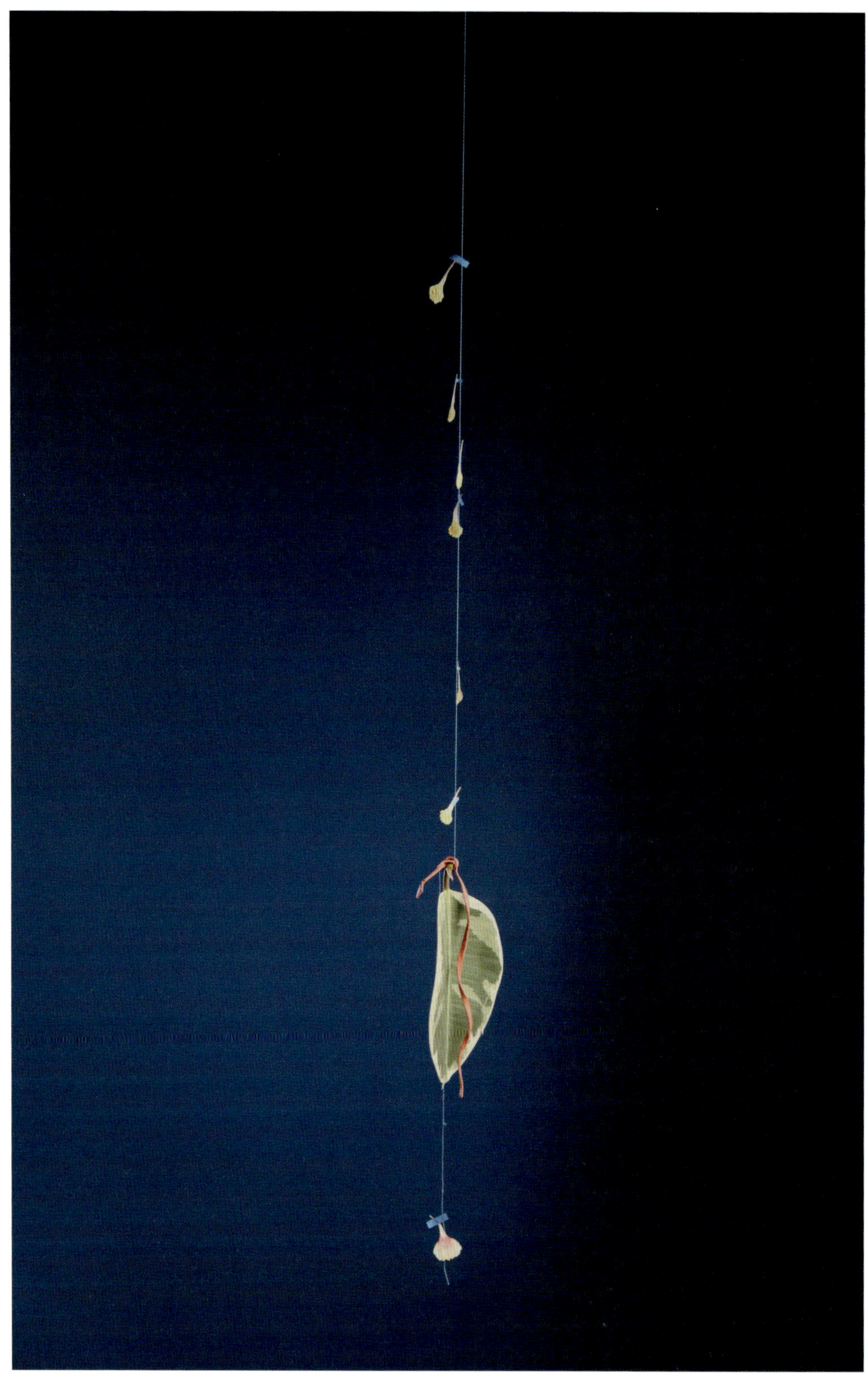

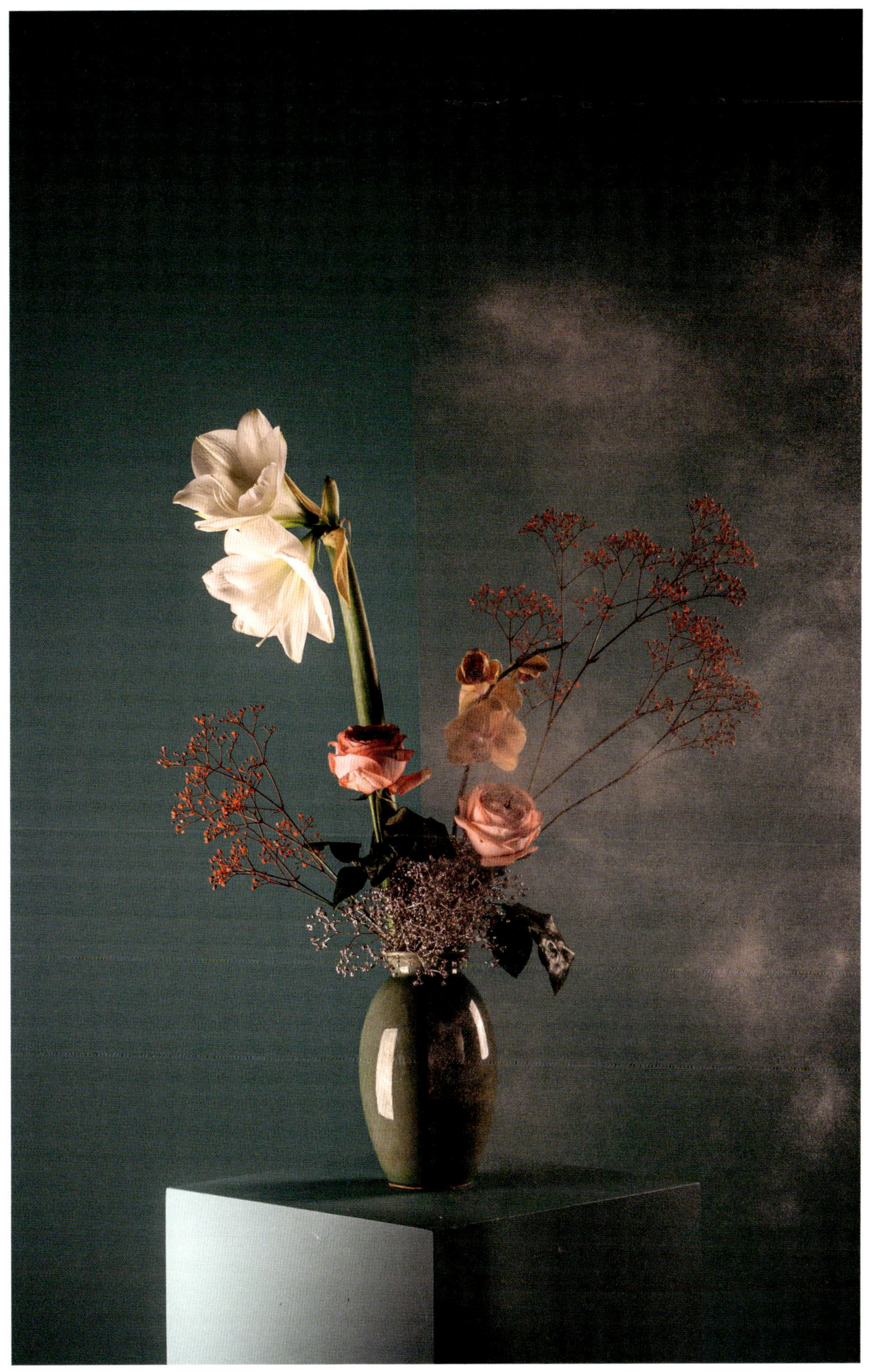

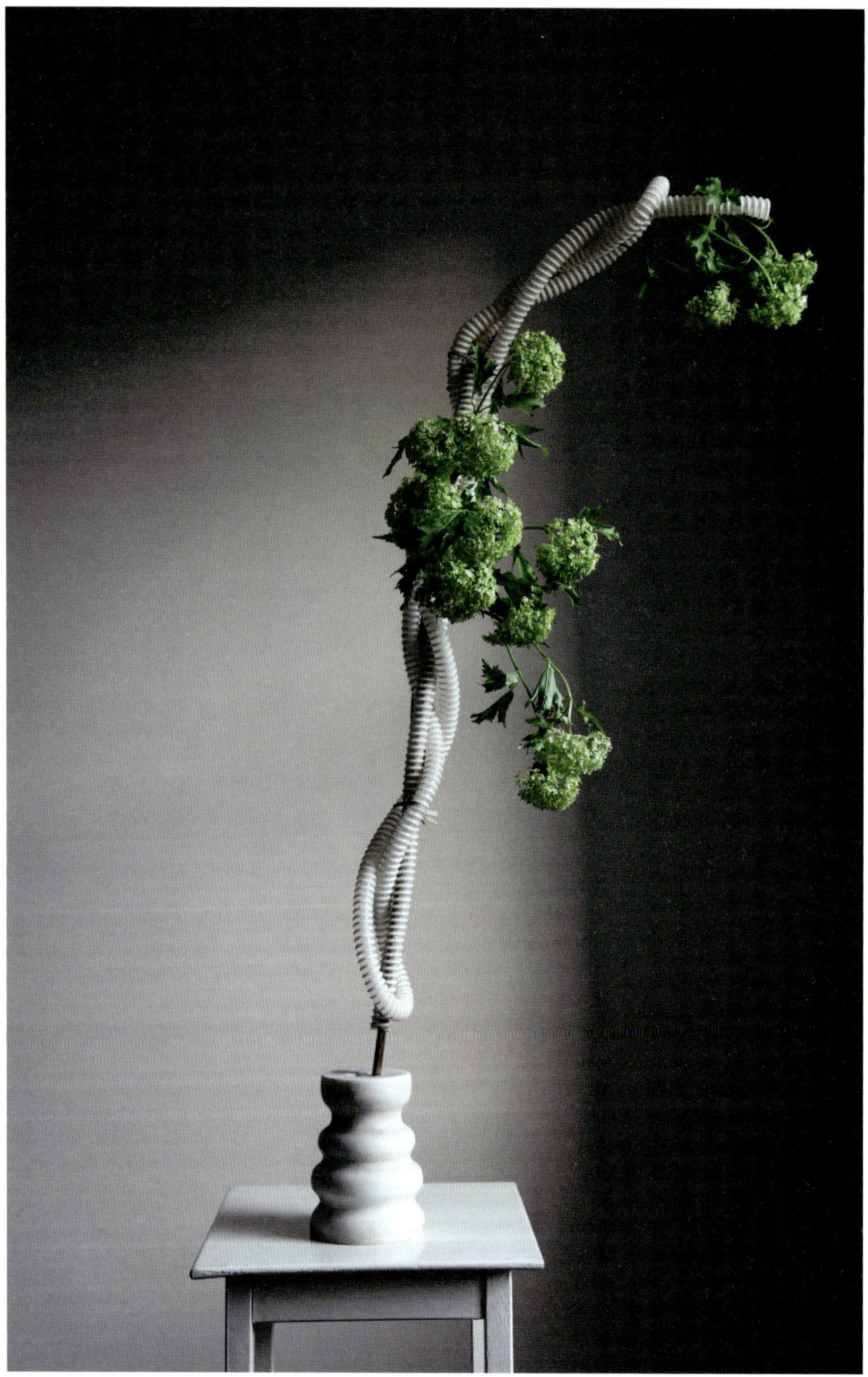

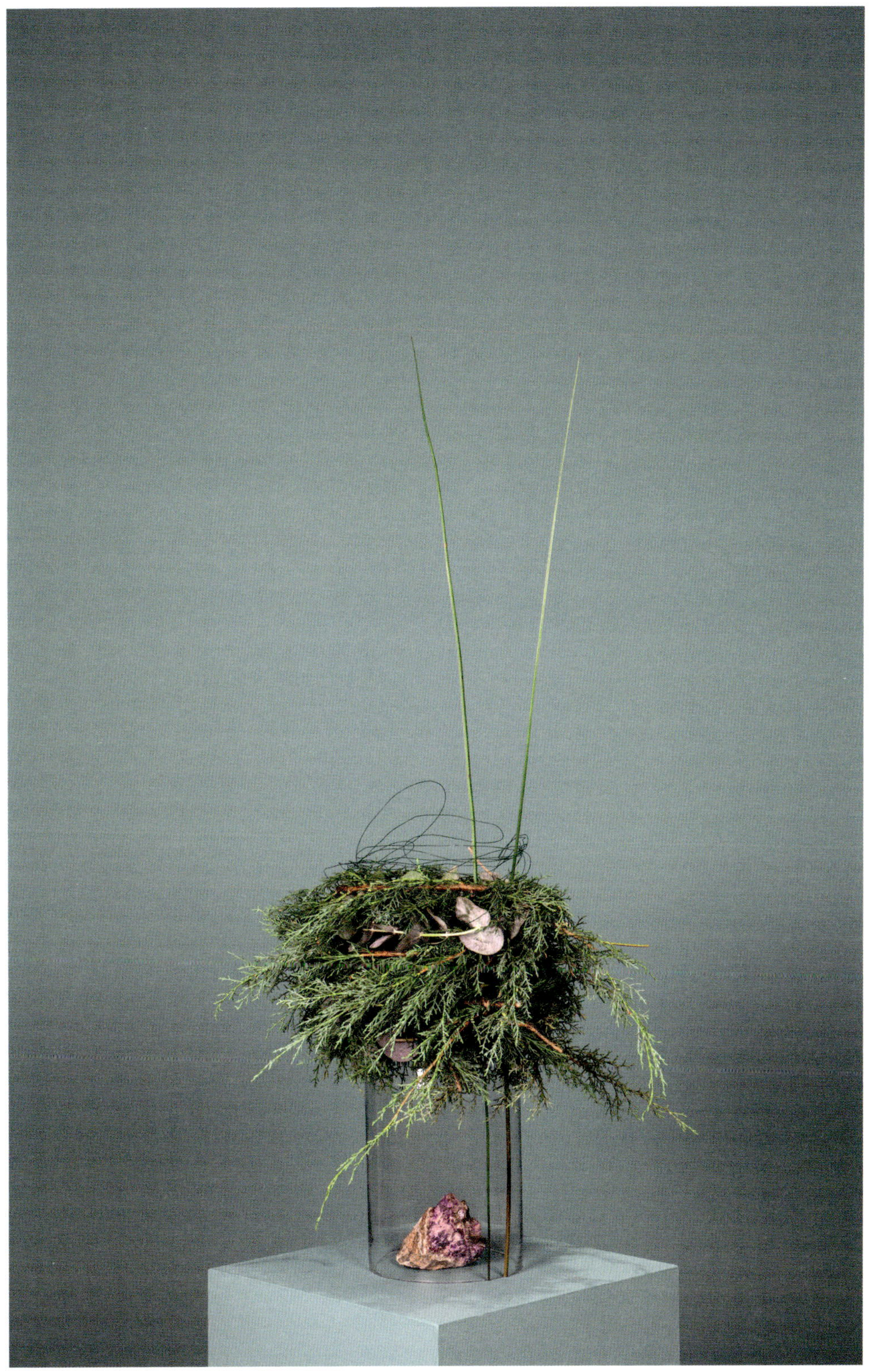

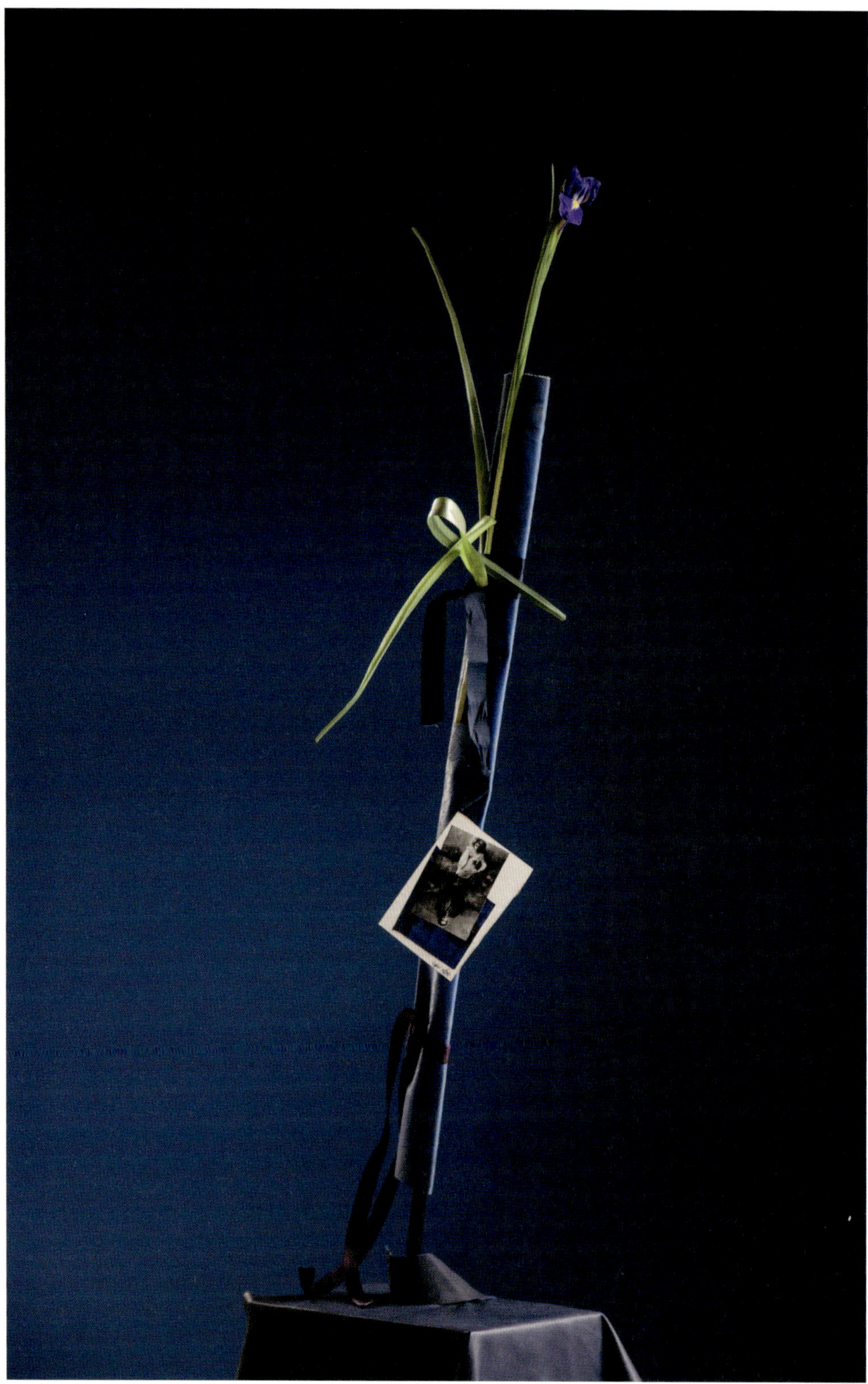

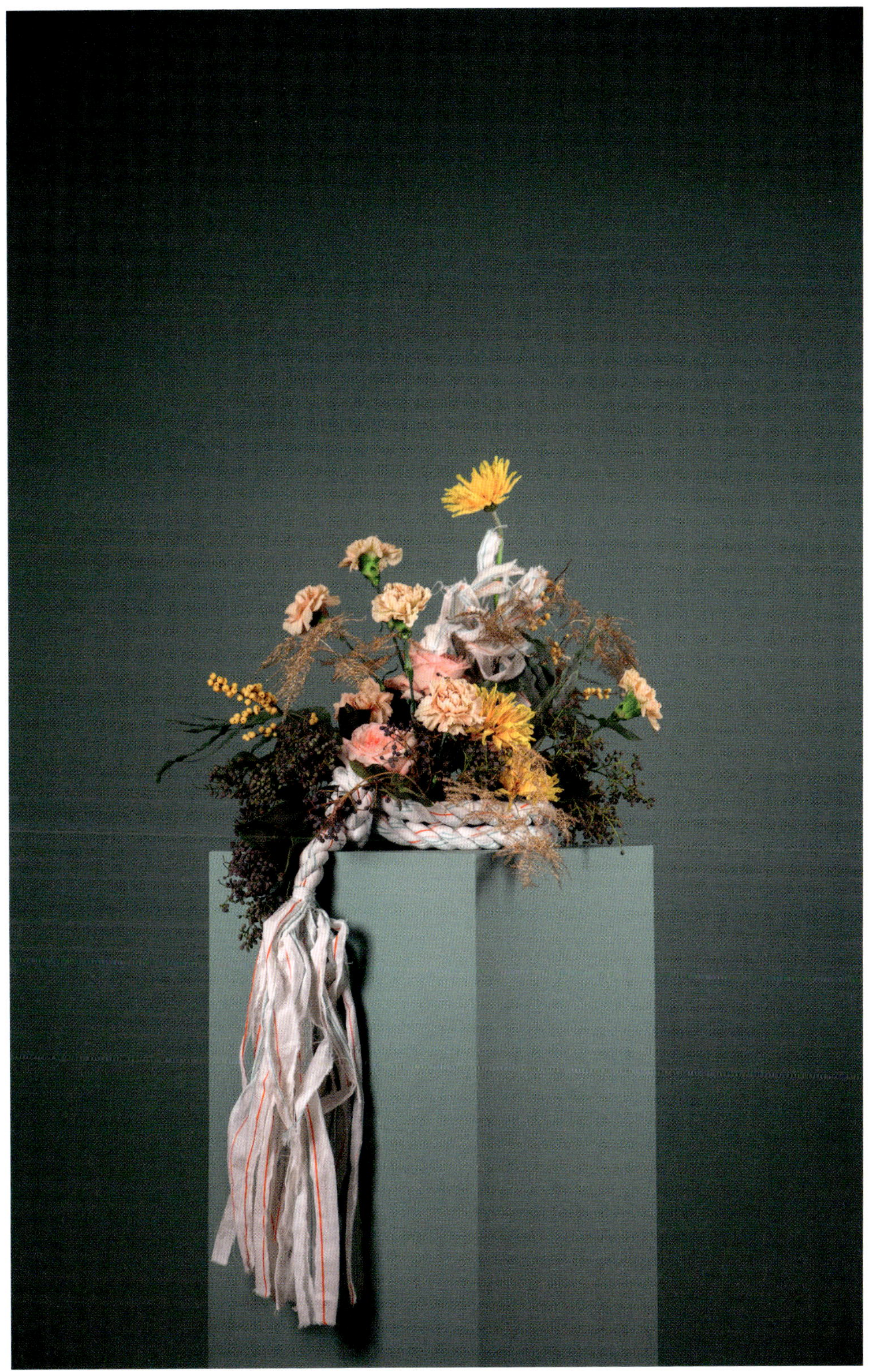

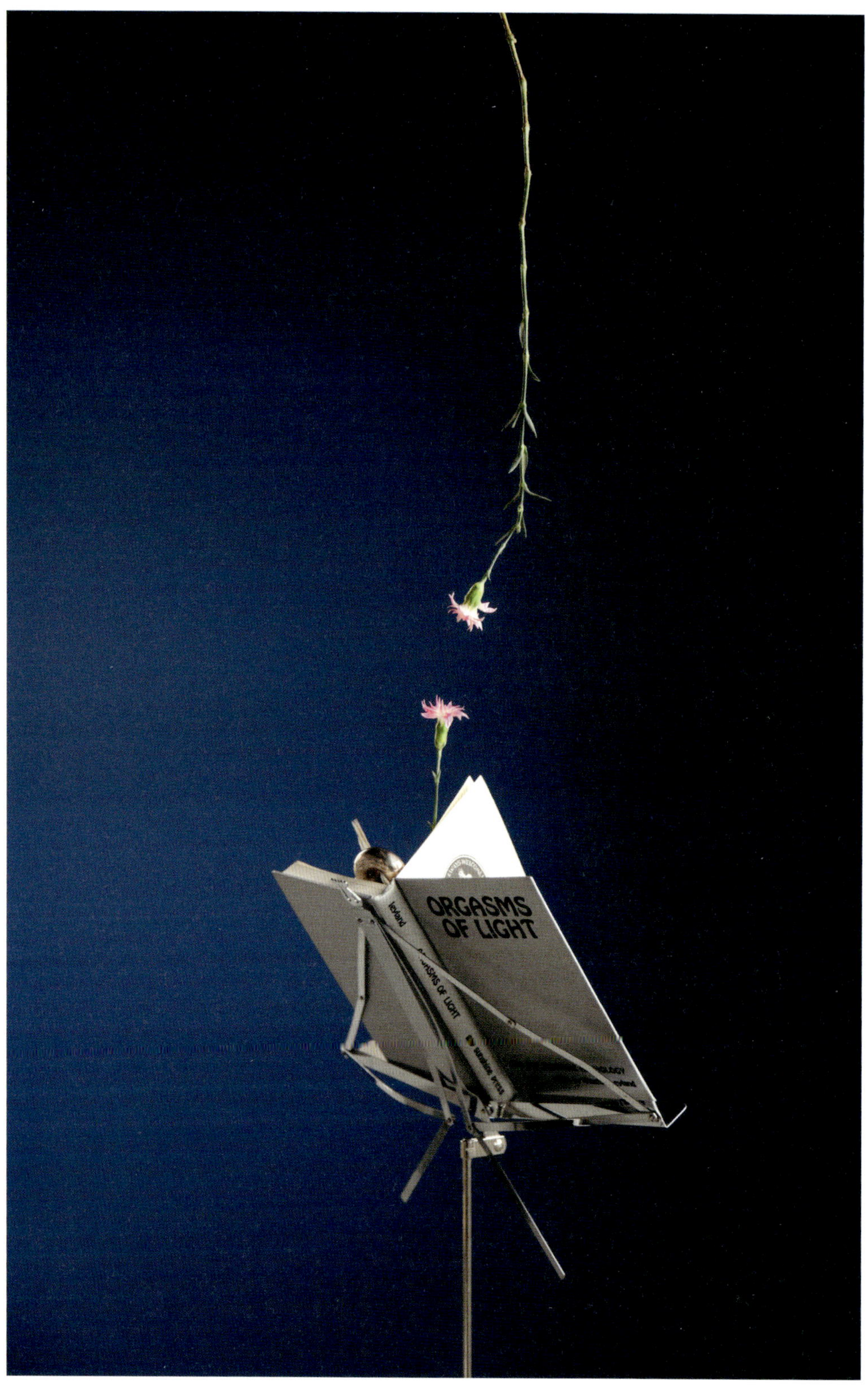
ORGASMS
OF LIGHT

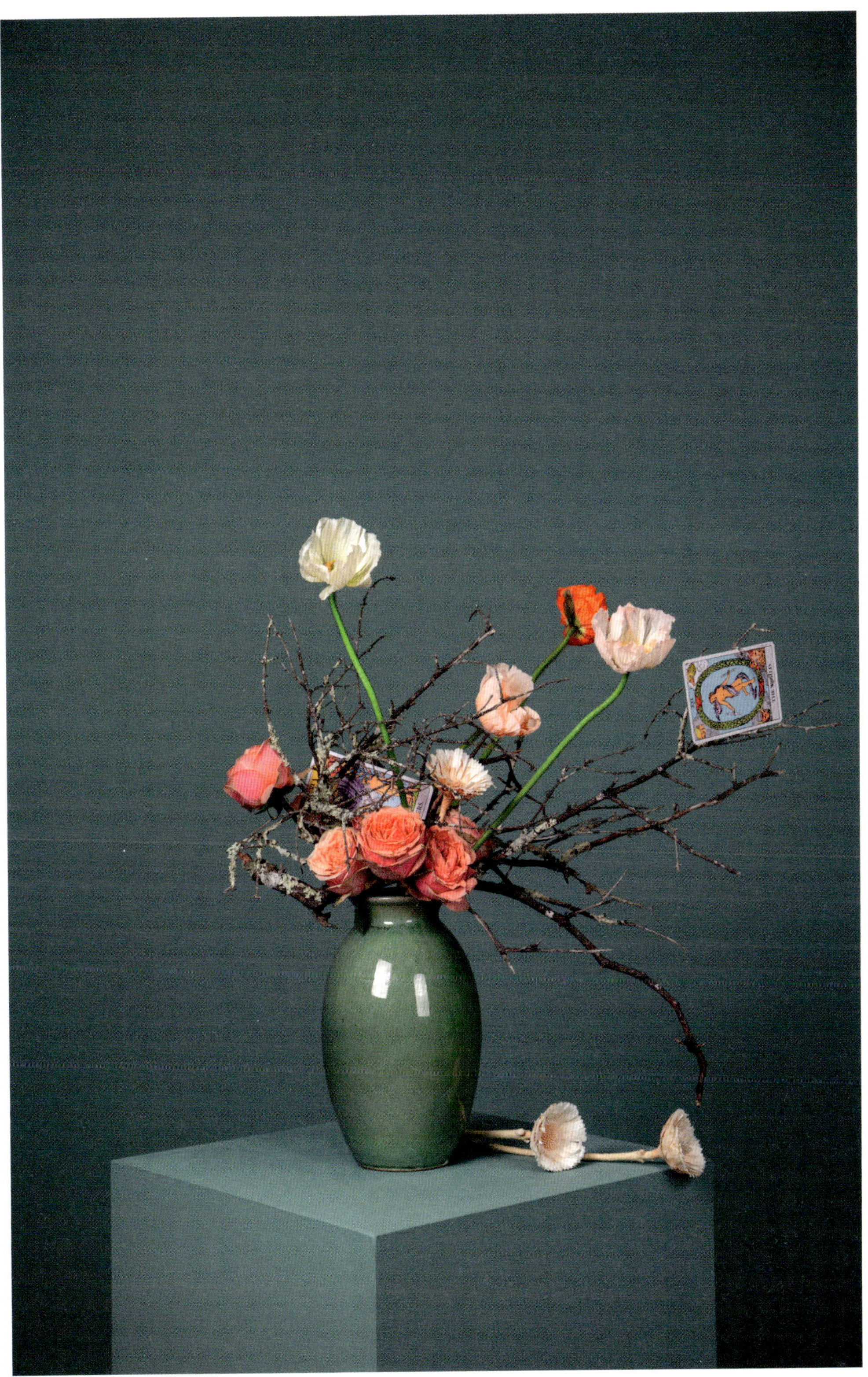

PLATES

Chapter 1

2 Benny Nemer, "A Hum in the Library," 2020. Ivy vines, leather, rose petals.

3 Vincent Edet in conversation with Kat Kosk, "The Wind Blows on the Dead and the Living," 2020. Spanish moss, dahlias, cymbidium orchids, ranunculus, foraged sticks, grass, woodbine. Photograph by Jason Laguerre.

Chapter 2

4 Benny Nemer, "A Line of Dutch Verse," 2020. Carnation, ribbon, leather, ceramic, shimmering text.

5 Vincent Edet in conversation with Kat Kosk, "The Clouds, They Hide Me," 2020. Foraged branches, cotton wired to sticks, dyed bunny tail grass. Photograph by Jason Laguerre.

Chapter 3

6 Benny Nemer, "A Portrait of Mattias as a Young Faggot," 2020. Gladiolas, Queen Anne's lace, a photograph of Mattias Duyves, c. 1975.

7 Vincent Edet in conversation with Kat Kosk, "A Capture in Time," 2020. Bamboo, Virginia creeper, Polaroid, shells. Photograph by Jason Laguerre.

Chapter 4

8 Benny Nemer, "An Octagonal Mirror," 2020. Chrysanthemum, mirror, plastic, leather.

9 Bill Brown and John McKinven in conversation with Kat Kosk, "You're Never Safe from Surprises," 2020. Roses, mullein, acetate, riding crop, cock ring. Photograph by Jason Laguerre.

Chapter 5

10 Benny Nemer, "Two Clocks," 2020. Clematis, rose and dahlia petals, leather, rubber, wire, mother of pearl. Photograph by Bastien Pourtout.

11 Bill Brown and John McKinven in conversation with Kat Kosk, "Sounds of Silence," 2020. Hydrangeas, chrysanthemums, bladder campion, clocks, duct tape, electrical tape. Photograph by Jason Laguerre.

Chapter 6

12 Benny Nemer, "A *Ficus drupacea pubescens*," 2020. Anthurium, gerbera, asparagus fern, lamb's ear, milkweed, the artist's body.

13 Lydia Collins in conversation with Kat Kosk, "Books Are Flowers," 2020. Calla, banksia, plumosa fern, eucalyptus, thyme, irises, dahlia, corn, grass, pine cones, flowers made from James Baldwin's *Notes of a Native Son*. Photograph by Jason Laguerre.

Chapter 7

14 Benny Nemer, "A Urinal," 2020. Metal, leather, chrysanthemum, dahlia and gerbera petals.

15 Lydia Collins in conversation with Kat Kosk, "The Stench of Romance," 2020. Roses, craspedia, wire. Photograph by Jason Laguerre.

Chapter 8

114 Benny Nemer, "Two Clock Towers," 2020. Dried Marseille campanula, leather, the artist's hand.

115 Lydia Collins in conversation with Kat Kosk, "We've Got Time," 2020. Pampas grass, steel grass, liguster berries. Photograph by Jason Laguerre.

Chapter 9

116 Benny Nemer, "A Feather Duster," 2020. Gaura blossoms, feathers, plastic, leather.

117 Benny Michaud in conversation with Kat Kosk, "Earth Blanket," 2020. Foraged woody vine, reindeer lichen, palapa. Photograph by Jason Laguerre.

Chapter 10

118 Benny Nemer, "Someone Is Weeping in the Library," 2020. Carnation petals, *Ficus elastica* "Variegata", leather, tape, thread.

119 Benny Michaud in conversation with Kat Kosk, "Distant Voices," 2020. Baby's breath, orchid, roses, amaryllis, cellophane, spray paint. Photograph by Jason Laguerre.

Chapter 11

120 Benny Nemer, "A Bathhouse," 2020. Viburnum, plastic tubing, leather, brass, an antique marble fixture from a Turkish hammam.

121 Sam Loewen in conversation with Kat Kosk, "An Aroma for an Aura," 2020. Carolina sapphire, amethyst crystal from the Bellevue Mine, baby eucalyptus, steel grass, wire. Photograph by Olivia Johnston.

Chapter 12

122 Benny Nemer, "A Postcard of a Still Life," 2020. Iris, ribbon, metal, plastic and a postcard dated April 1996 handmade by the artist's grandmother, Rosalie Goodman Namer (1925-2006), using a magazine clipping, cardboard and glue.

123 Sam Loewen in conversation with Kat Kosk, "Trouser Snake," 2020. O'Hara garden roses, carnations, gerbera, ilex, asparagus plumosa, liguster berries, fern, handspun bedsheet rope. Photograph by Olivia Johnston.

Chapter 13

124 Benny Nemer, "An Ex Libris Label," 2020. Mini carnations, leather, flute mouthpiece, music stand, copy of *Orgasms of Light* (1978) published by Gay Sunshine Press.

125 Sam Loewen in conversation with Kat Kosk, "The World Will Always Welcome Lovers," 2020. Icelandic poppies, roses, lichen cedar, the Lovers and the World (reversed) tarot cards, unidentified white spider, unidentified dried flowers. Photograph by Olivia Johnston.

Unless otherwise indicated, photographs of floral arrangements are by Benny Nemer.

This publication documents the exhibition *Benny Nemer: I Don't Know Where Paradise Is*, curated by Heather Anderson and presented at Carleton University Art Gallery from September 24 to December 12, 2020.

Library and Archives Canada Cataloguing in Publication

Title
Benny Nemer: *I don't know where paradise is / texts by Heather Anderson, Jennifer Evans, Ann Cvetkovich, John Potvin*. Other titles: *I don't know where paradise is*

Names
Container of (work): Nemer, Benny, 1973–Works. Selections. Carleton University. Art Gallery, host institution, publisher.

Description
Includes texts by Jennifer Evans, Ann Cvetkovich, John Potvin, Benny Nemer. Catalogue of the exhibition Benny Nemer: I Don't Know Where Paradise Is, held at the Carleton University Art Gallery from September 24 to December 12, 2020. Includes bibliographical references.

Identifiers
Canadiana 2023021956X
ISBN 9781488400339 (hardcover)

Subjects
LCSH: Nemer, Benny, 1973–Exhibitions.
LCGFT: Exhibition catalogs.

Classification
LCC N6549.N46 A4 2023
DDC 709.2–dc23

General editors and project managers
Heather Anderson and Benny Nemer

Editors
Meg Taylor and Ruth Gaskill

Graphic design
Clément Wibaut, Paris

Pre-press
Fotimprim, Paris

Printed by
Média Graphic, Rennes

Paper
Wibalin Buckram (cover)
Tintoretto Ceylon Sesamo (end pages)
Arena Natural Bulk (texts)
Symbol Tatami (plates)

Typefaces
Garamond Premier and Optima

This publication is supported generously by Carleton University, the Canada Council for the Arts and the Ontario Arts Council, an Ontario government agency

© Carleton University Art Gallery, 2023. All rights reserved. Reproduction in any form without prior written permission is prohibited.

Legal Deposit, Library and Archives Canada, 2023

Carleton University Art Gallery
St. Patrick's Building, Carleton University
1125 Colonel By Drive
Ottawa, ON, Canada K1S 5B6
cuag.ca | +1 613-520-2120

cuag Carleton University Art Gallery

Carleton University

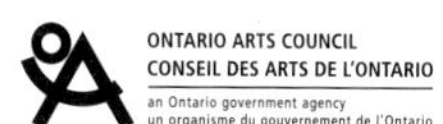

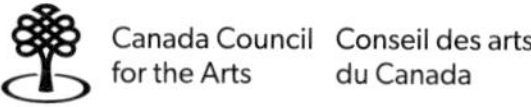

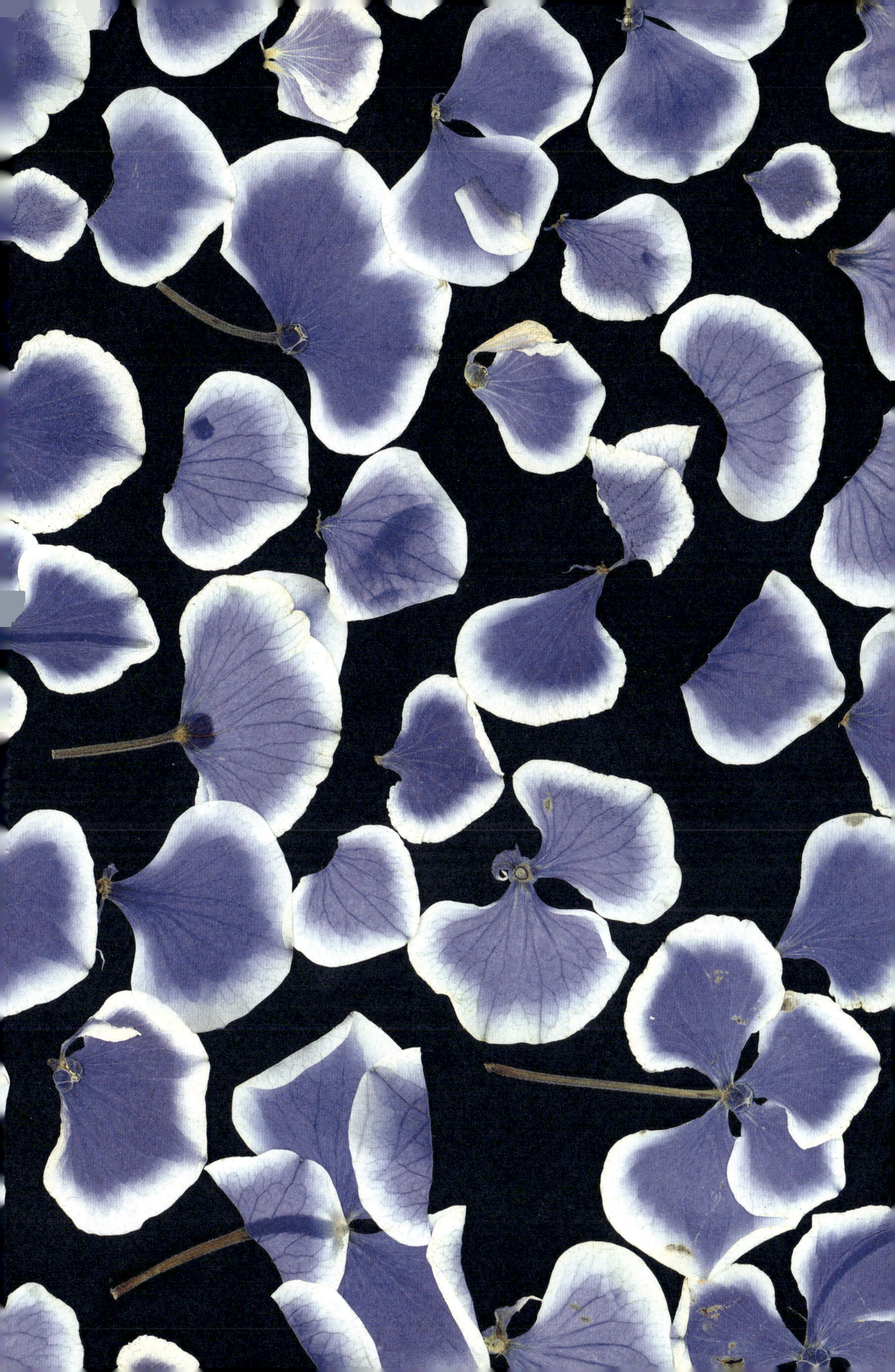

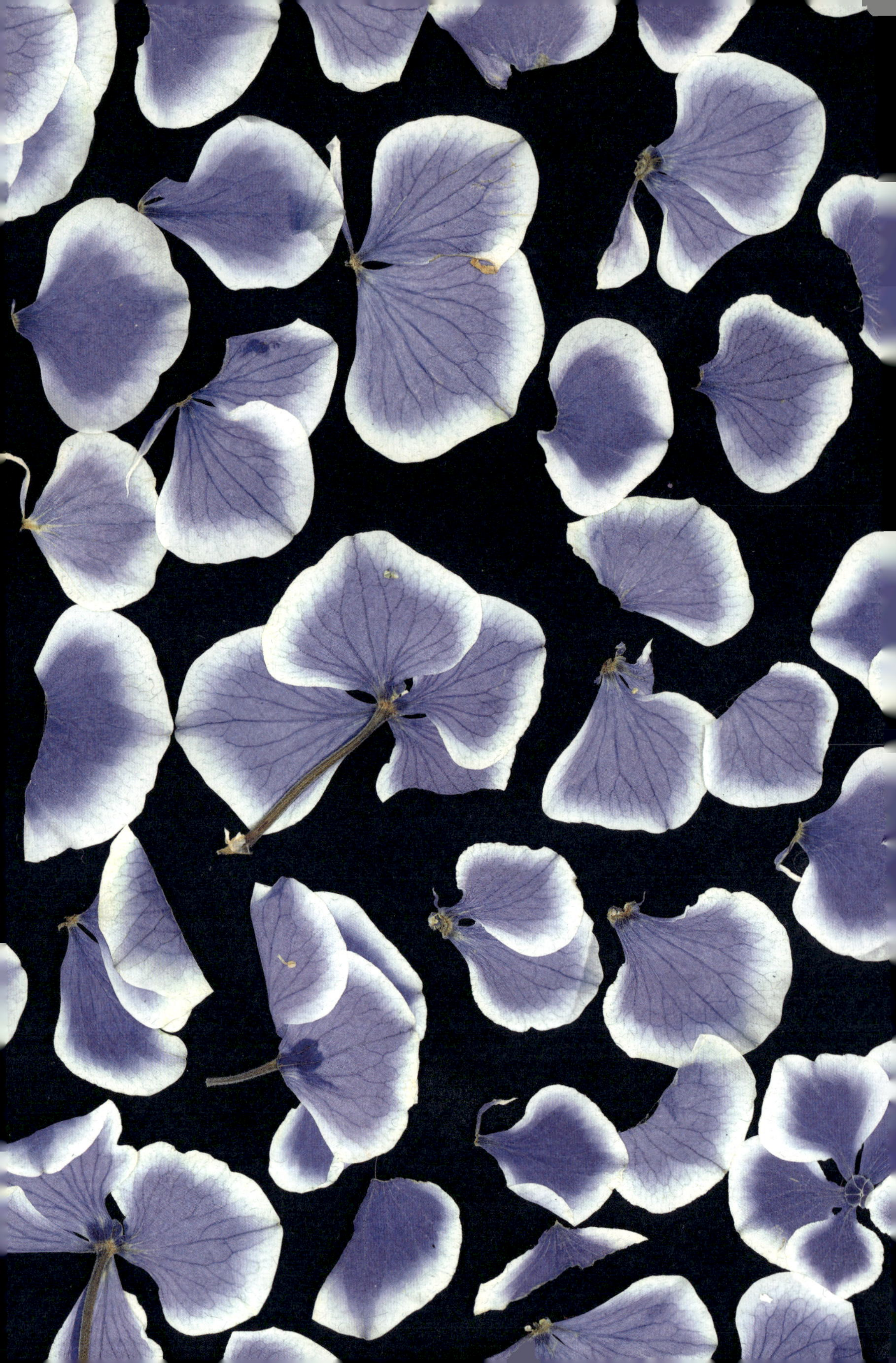